YOU
CAN BE A
SON

Secret of Eternity

To Open Their Eyes

Steven & Bonnie Moore

You Can Be a Son, Secret of Eternity
Printed in the United States of America
ISBN: 978-1-63599-000-3

© Copyright 2017 – Steven and Bonnie Moore
2608 West Kenosha Suite 220 - Broken Arrow, OK 74012
Email: truthforeternity@live.com Website: truthforeternity.com

This book is available through local bookstores and amazon.com in print and eBook.

Contents

Preface

Hast thou heard the secret of God?

Have you not heard? Do you not know? God has a secret and He wants to share it with you. The secret of eternity lies hidden in the Scriptures, but it is revealed to those who love God and want to know His wisdom.

The secret of eternity will affect you forever, either in a positive way or in a negative way. It will depend upon you. What is the difference between ignorance and a lie? Nothing! They both produce the same results. In both cases one fails to partake of what rightfully belongs to him.

> But we speak the wisdom of God in a mystery, the hidden wisdom which God ordained before the ages for our glory, which none of the rulers of this age knew; for had they known, they would not have crucified the Lord of glory. (1 Cor. 2:7,8 NKJV)

The Bible is a love letter sent down from Heaven with a glorious revelation sealed inside. Those that humble themselves and unlock the Heavenly seal will learn the secret of eternity that lies hidden within the Bible. This book is like a Bible school course in a book. It opens the eyes to reveal many common deceptions and areas of ignorance. It is a methodical foundational book that will help people from all walks of life to easily understand the Bible. The teachings of the Bible revolve around one major theme and that theme is the true incentive of the Bible and the purpose for which God wrote it. After reading this book you will be able to study the Bible for yourself and comprehend the wisdom of God in a mystery.

For two thousand years, the teachings of the traditional Church have centered on the forgiveness of sins and Heaven when we die. This has left the worldwide church weak and beggarly in its knowledge and character. God is doing much more for us than just forgiving our sins and taking us to Heaven when we die. Little do we imagine God forgiving us of everything we've ever done wrong forever because the natural mind is usually focused upon the here and now. However, the Bible is a supernatural book that releases supernatural power from God into the hearts and minds of humans. In this book, you will behold the hope and purpose of every soul ever born. God will show you great and mighty things, which you know not.

> For I consider that the sufferings of this present time are not worthy to be compared with the glory, which shall be revealed in us. For the earnest expectation of the creation eagerly waits for the revealing of the sons of God. For the creation was subjected to futility, not willingly, but because of Him who subjected it in hope; because the creation itself also will be delivered from the bondage of corruption into the glorious liberty of the children of God. For we know that *the whole creation groans and labors with birth pangs* together until now. (Rom. 8:18-22 NKJV)

The Bible says the whole universe is groaning in pain and crying out for the power of God to come to its rescue. What God is about to reveal to our world is beyond the imagination of man. It's supernatural. It is *not* of this world. Yet it has been in the pages of the Bible all along. God is doing something so wonderful, it cannot be compared to worldly things. It is the purpose of creation. It is the reason we exist.

> Call to me, and I will answer you, and show you great and mighty things, which you do not know. (Jer. 33:3 NKJV)

Have you ever wondered what the Bible is all about? Have you ever thought, "The Bible is such a big book and I just don't know where to start"? If so, you are not alone. There is a secret in the Bible that opens your eyes to the things of the spiritual realm. It lies hidden in every book of the Bible. As you read this book, you will progressively see God's purpose for creation, the human problem, God's solution, how God implements His solution with supernatural power and how it affects you forever. You will come to know the secret of eternity. For too long we have settled for forgiveness of sins and Heaven when we die, but there is so much more that God wants to show us. The Bible is not just a belief system. It's a revelation of the power of God. Yet we must believe it to see it and understand it.

> Blessed be the God and Father of our Lord Jesus Christ, who according to His abundant mercy has begotten us again to a living hope through the resurrection of Jesus Christ from the dead, to an inheritance incorruptible and undefiled and that does not fade away, reserved in heaven for you, who are kept by the power of God through faith for salvation ready to be revealed in the last time. (1 Pet. 1:3-5 NKJV)

The secret of eternity reveals God's eternal perspective in the Bible. Forgiveness of sins and Heaven when we die are only the beginning of God's love and provision for you. God wants to show us the true incentive of His eternal plan so we can walk in the power of God while we are on earth.

> Take heed, brethren, lest there be in any of you an evil heart of unbelief, in departing from the living God. But exhort one another daily, while it is called today, lest any of you be hardened through the deceitfulness of sin. For we are made partakers of Christ, if we hold the beginning of our confidence stedfast unto the end; While it is said, today if ye will hear his voice, harden not your hearts, as in the provocation. (Heb. 3:12-15)

CHAPTER 1

TIME *and* ETERNITY

A good name is better than precious ointment;
and the day of death than the day of one's birth.

ECCLES. 7:1

The two greatest days in one's life are the day of one's birth and the day of one's death. The Bible says the day of one's death is greater than the day of one's birth.

With humans, time is normal, but with God, eternity is normal. Birth is a magnificent thing, but the day of death is the day we enter into our eternal destiny.

Of course, for those who are going to Heaven the day of one's death is greater than one's birth. God didn't create us to have a party on planet Earth for a few moments of time. God is very exact and He had a precise reason for creating us.

God wrote the Bible to help us understand His purpose for creating the universe and to answer our questions so we can make an intelligent decision ahead of *time*. If you are wise you will benefit greatly from what God has prepared for you before you were born.

The natural mind of man sees life like a storybook, which has a beginning and an end, but God thinks with the mindset of forever. Natural birth brings us into the earth realm for a time, but the day of one's death is when the natural human enters his destiny for eternity.

That day when your destiny becomes final could be today. One day the truth of life and death will surely become reality for you and understanding will be a necessity for you. Don't you think it would be wise to address the issues of eternity before it is too late and you are caught by surprise?

Or do you take the attitude of eat, drink, and be merry for tomorrow we die? God cautions us in the Bible to not take things for granted. God wants truth to be reality for you now and He wants you to be ready when that day comes.

In college when the professor gave us a little more time to get the correct answers on the test, we were glad. God has done that with time. We are given the opportunity to get ready for eternity. Then when that day comes, how many people are ready? How about you, are you ready? For believers, eternity has already begun.

> The Lord is not slack concerning His promise, as some men count slackness; but is longsuffering to us, not willing that any should perish, but that all should come to repentance. (2 Pet. 3:9 NKJV)

The Bible is clear God doesn't want anyone to perish. However, the Bible says a lot of people will perish. What separates you from everybody else? God wrote the Bible to help you understand that. The Bible says God is the living God. He is a personal God who wants everyone to live and win in life. In the Bible, God tells you how He has made it possible for you to live in victory and then live forever.

> Whereas you do not know what shall happen tomorrow. For what is your life? It is even a vapor that appears for a little time, and then vanishes away. (Jas. 4:14 NKJV)

No matter what you are going through in life, destiny awaits you. No matter how good things have been, and no matter how bad things are going, destiny awaits you. Soon and very soon your time will end, this world will pass away, and eternity will begin for you. Time flies away like a bird. Scripture says your life is like a vapor, which appears for a short time and then vanishes away. How often do you think like that? Are you prepared? As I, Steven, wrote this book, I became concerned that what you are about to read might be too much for some. But if today is your last day on earth, I think it will be barely enough.

This isn't one of those little books that will make you feel good for a few minutes. This book will *challenge you, encourage you, and comfort you*. It will make you think about the issues of life and death. We might not even be here tomorrow. The Bible doesn't promise us tomorrow. But the Bible does make some incredible promises to those who can believe them. The Bible is a supernatural book that imparts supernatural power to humans. If you can understand the Bible with your heart, it will change your life.

> For we know in part and we prophesy in part. But when that which is perfect has come, then that which is in part will be done away. When I was a child, I spoke as a child, I understood as a child, I thought as a child; but when I became a man, I put away childish things. For now, we see in a mirror, dimly, but then face to face. Now I know in part, but then I shall know just as I also am known. (1 Cor. 13:9-12 NKJV)

We are all building an eternal house, and thoughts on truth are the steel beams that will hold up our house forever. God wants us to see the true incentive of the Bible and to know the *Truth of Eternity* before it is too late. It is easier to face the truth than it is to face death without knowing the truth. Going into eternity without truth is like throwing a baby into the ocean and shouting, "Swim!" In the day of death, without truth, you will drown forever. It is easier to face death when you know the truth.

This book maintains a unique intensity and repetition that simplifies the Bible. This kind of intensity is nothing compared to the intensity of facing death without knowing truth. God wrote the Bible to show us the truth. I believe there are three main truths the Creator wants the creature to know that focus on your spirit, your soul, and your body. The first few chapters will be a little slow but they set the reader up to see these three main truths and understand the true incentive of the Bible. As you read the scriptures, look at which parts they are focused upon. This following scripture is a good example:

> And the very God of peace sanctify you wholly; and I pray God your whole spirit and soul and body be preserved blameless unto the coming of our Lord Jesus Christ. (1 Thess. 5:23)

Look to see how God is dividing things. This scripture divides the human by spirit, soul and body. God divides time into past, present and future. The renewing of our mind helps to give us the ability to make adjustments to the area in need, spirit, soul or body. God wants to transform us from what we are into what He created us to be. Also reading the scriptures out loud helps to see God's perspective. What you don't understand you will lose. In every scripture, try to see the secret God wants to reveal to you.

> Jesus answered and said unto them, Ye do err, not knowing the scriptures, nor the power of God. (Matt. 22:29)

Through the Bible God teaches us about His purpose for creation, about the processes of time and seasons, about life and death, and of eternity. We enter into earth as a natural being and we are supposed to leave planet Earth as a spiritual being, prepared for Heaven. True spirituality from God's perspective in the Bible is diametrically opposed to the ideas of religion. The Bible will open your heart and your mind with truth for eternity, and then you will see from the eternal perspective that what God is doing is perfectly normal and natural. As understanding comes, wisdom will begin, the power of God will flow and God will be pleased to show off for you.

The Marvel of the Bible

Behold ye among the nations, and look, and wonder marvelously; for I am working a work in your days, which ye will not believe though it be told you. (Hab. 1:5)

What the Bible wants to reveal to us is not of this world. God has literally reached down out of Heaven to show us all something so marvelous it is beyond our imagination. As you read this book you will see what love is and what God, in His love, has done for you. No religion created by man or angel can compare or even come close to the wisdom of God. What God is doing can't be understood by the natural mind. God has to reveal it to us. However, what God shows us He is doing in the Bible makes perfect natural sense to the spiritual man. It is the hidden wisdom of God in a mystery.

The stone, which the builders rejected, has become the chief cornerstone. This was the LORD's doing; it is marvelous in our eyes. (Ps. 118:22-23 NKJV)

Why is it that many people find the Bible hard to understand? That is part of the secret of the Bible you will learn in this book. The Bible isn't like any other book. To truly understand the Bible, God has to open our eyes to see truth. Before we can even see truth in the Bible, God has to do something in our hearts to make us ready.

The Bible is like
✓ A Love Letter from a long-lost unknown Father
✓ A Book of Secrets hidden behind a puzzle painting
✓ A Treasure Chest full of priceless treasures
✓ An Owner's Manual to put the pieces back together
✓ A Hidden Door inside a closet that becomes a portal into another world

> But the natural man does not receive the things of the Spirit of God, for they are foolishness unto him: nor can he know them, because they are spiritually discerned. (1 Cor. 2:14)

The Bible is a *living book* that imparts God's Spirit to the human. God has written the Bible for all generations. Some truths are reserved for each generation and have been locked up for thousands of years, just waiting for each generation to come. God is doing something only God can do and it is wonderfully marvelous. It is beyond our imagination.

> But as it is written, Eye has not seen, nor ear heard, nor have entered into the heart of man, the things which God hath prepared for them that love him. But God has revealed them unto us through his Spirit: for the Spirit searches all things, yes, the deep things of God. (1 Cor. 2:9-11 NKJV)

When you truly know the secret of eternity, you can understand the message of the Bible. However, God reveals these things to us by His Spirit when our hearts are right. Even when we think we do understand the Bible, we will find we've only touched the tip of the iceberg and there is still so much more. God's revelation only comes through the heart, by His Holy Spirit. The two scriptures above show us the natural man who lives for and follows after the things of the flesh cannot receive the things of the Spirit.

> For those who live according to the Flesh set their minds on the things of the flesh; but they that live according to the Spirit the things of the Spirit. For to be carnally minded is death; but to be spiritually minded is life and peace. Because the carnal mind is enmity against God: for it is not subject to the law of God, neither indeed can be. (Rom. 8:5-7 NKJV)

The mind of the natural man is *against* God. Therefore, he cannot spiritually discern the things of the Spirit, so God must open his eyes. God wrote the Bible to show us His perspective. God wants every soul to know the truth that will last for all eternity. There is a common theme, a familiar voice, a single focus, and a sure foundation that runs throughout the whole Bible that God wants to reveal to our hearts and minds. The *Truth for Eternity* is the theme of the Bible and God wants to show it to us in every page.

> Laying up in store for themselves a good foundation against the time to come, that they may lay hold on eternal life. (1 Tim. 6:19)

Whether you decide to believe the Bible or not is the decision you alone have to make. If your heart is after everything this world has to offer, you might miss what God is offering you for eternity. Your natural mind may have more important things to do than decide what you believe in life. The most important thing to prepare for in life is death!

From the day we are born we are headed toward that day when everything becomes final and eternal. You can only put off the issues of eternity for so long. We are not promised tomorrow. One day you will die and what happens to you after that will depend on how you responded to God's message to you in His book called the Bible. If your foundation of what you believe isn't right, your eternity isn't safe. Through the scriptures God exhorts us to lay up for ourselves *a good foundation against the time to come*, and *to lay hold on eternal life*. God has been preparing things for you for thousands of years and He sent Jesus to make these things possible for you.

How have you responded to God? When you find out what God has prepared for you before you were born, you will think it is impossible. The good news of the Bible is, all things are possible with God. He has already done everything without our help. That is something no mere religion can offer. When eternity comes, it's forever. The only thing that will matter then is, do you believe what God has said? Are you ready and are you safe? Did you get ready while you were on earth? If not, you will wish you were never born.

The God of the Bible

> Can any man by searching find out God? Can he find out the Almighty unto perfection? It is as high as heaven; what can he do? Deeper than Hell and the grave; what can he know? (Job 11:7-8)

As a young man I searched for years for the truth of life and death. In my early twenties, living in California, I studied the religions of the world until I was burned out. Then one day I was in my bedroom, by myself, lying on the bed and talking to God. I was saying from my heart, "God, if you are real, then I want to know you. I know all these religions are not what I'm looking for. I want to know the truth about life and death and eternity." God responded!

As I lay there pondering as far back as I could remember, God took me back in my memory to my grandmother. She was the one person who I knew really loved me as a child and I loved my grandma. When I went to her house as a kid, I felt loved. Her love was a love I have never seen or felt in anyone else. She loved Jesus and she was like Jesus in all her ways. She always talked to me about Him. She loved me and as far as I know she prayed for me every day of my life. As God reminded me of her, first I saw her face, then I saw her eyes, and the love of Jesus in her eyes. Then I saw Jesus *in her*, and all of a sudden, there He was, standing in my bedroom with His arms stretched out wide and I knew He loved me. I was shocked, excited, and overwhelmed. In that moment of my excitement He was gone. Then I was shocked and disappointed because He was gone. I knew right then that Jesus was real and He loved me. It was clear to me the God I wanted to know was my grandma's God, the God of love.

I wondered why I studied most of the religions of the world but never considered the Bible. The one thing all the religions lacked was the love of God. What my heart was looking for I couldn't find in all those religions. I could only see it in Jesus. That day I realized there is something on the inside of the human spirit that cannot be satisfied without the love of God. When you know in your heart you are loved by God, you know you are safe forever and peace flows like a river. Your spirit knows nothing is greater than God. Your spirit knows nothing can separate you from the love of God. Until my heart was ignited by love, I was no better than any unbelieving atheist. No matter how much searching I did, I was as ignorant as a rock. No matter how hard I searched, I still couldn't find what I was looking for. Gaining knowledge feels good, but knowledge alone doesn't have the love of God or the life of God in it.

Scientific tests have been done on the biblical texts of the Old Testament. The letters of the Hebrew alphabet are also used as numbers.

These tests have confirmed through mathematical science that the language of the Bible has the same numerical formula throughout the Old Testament. These tests provide scientific proof the books of the Bible were written by the same author. This is impossible in the natural world because these documents, which form the books of the Bible, were written through many different humans over a period of two thousand years. Humans only live so long, but God isn't limited by time. With God all things are possible. God kept writing His book throughout the centuries to tell us the truth and to show us the truth. The Bible bears witness of itself as to how the Bible was written.

> And so we have the prophetic word confirmed, which you do well to heed as a light that shines in a dark place, until the day dawns, and the morning star rises in your hearts; knowing this first, that no prophecy of the Scripture is of any private interpretation, for prophecy never came by the will of man, but holy men of God spoke as they were moved by the Holy Spirit. (2 Pet. 1:19-21 NKJV)

Holy people who walked with God, and were separated unto God, were moved by God's Spirit to speak words that came to them from God. These words of God were written down and preserved as books of the Bible. God isn't limited by time. God has been walking in our midst from the cradle of the human race until this present time and He will be with us in our next generation, even until time ends and eternity continues. God isn't going anywhere. We humans think in the context of time, but God does not. God has been with the human race from the beginning. And He also has been with you. God has been with you from the day you were born and He will be with you until the day you die. If you don't know God is with you, then you don't benefit as much. It's as if someone left you an inheritance and you don't know about it. Even though the inheritance belongs to you, it doesn't benefit you. If you can't see God when He is working in your life, it won't benefit you. You may just call it a feeling, a hunch, or a coincidence.

God can do more for you in thirty seconds than you can do in your whole life. In the day of death, you will enter into eternity and go on to your eternal destination, and God will respect the choices you have made.

If you have chosen to walk with God in your life, your walk with God will continue for eternity. If you have chosen to live life without God, your existence without God will continue for eternity. God wrote the Bible to bring us back to Him.

From the natural perspective the Bible shows us history. From the spiritual perspective the Bible reveals His-story. The Bible documents the window of time that God cut out of eternity to walk with man and develop an eternal family. As you observe God's walk through time in the Bible, you'll see God isn't in a hurry and He isn't making any mistakes. He knows everything that will happen before time and He even tells us ahead of time. Humans come and go, but God continues His walk through time, doing His will and accomplishing His purpose. God documents all His events and activities in the Bible, before and after they happen, for our instruction. You can watch God walk through time in the Bible, but until you connect with God in your heart, it is too high for your natural mind.

> For my thoughts are not your thoughts, neither are your ways my ways, saith the LORD. For as the heavens are higher than the earth, so are my ways higher than your ways, and my thoughts than your thoughts. (Isa. 55:8-9)

Our five senses were designed to take in earthly information. We need more than that to comprehend God's ways in the Bible. Our ways flow out of our thoughts. God's ways demonstrate God's thoughts. We can't walk with God in life without coming into agreement with Him. His wisdom is much higher than ours and our minds alone cannot comprehend His thoughts. Also, our hearts are wicked in His sight so without His help it is impossible to come into agreement with Him.

> The heart is deceitful above all things, and desperately wicked: who can know it? (Jer. 17:9)

God connects Spirit to spirit with us. Our spirit is a distinct section of our heart. Our heart is the seat of our soul, which is made up of our mind, will, intellect and emotions. God can only be known in our spirit. God is a Spirit and we have to connect with Him, spirit to Spirit. Our spirit affects the believing of our heart. We believe things with our hearts. Then our hearts go to work on our minds, intellects and emotions to enforce those beliefs with corresponding actions, deeds and words. We all have set some boundaries in our hearts that we live by. We all have set some officiating beliefs and have made inner vows that referee what's going on in our minds. Inner vows are things like, "I will not be like my dad," or "I will never get married." Officiating beliefs are things like, "He's my friend if he agrees with me" or "I will only vote for the candidate of my political party," etc. We have all determined some officiating beliefs that result in actions taken or not taken. The Bible says *the heart is deceitful above all things, desperately wicked, how can we know it?* So if we want things to change, we must change. For example, God said, "Thou shalt not lie." Then you have to come to the place where change begins and you take action to stop lying. Sure you will fall sometimes, but you get back up by repenting (telling God you are sorry), and then you live by the new standard that you set in the control room of your heart. Someone said, "You need a check-up from the neck-up." That sounds good but with God you have to "start with your heart to get a fresh start and see wickedness depart."

Can two walk together, except they be agreed? (Amos 3:3)

Revelation knowledge comes from God through the Bible, as His words are quickened and made alive, by His Spirit to our spirit inside our heart. The God of the Bible is a personal God who talks to our spirit. That's the part of us that will live forever. Yet it is His pleasure to reveal Himself to us when we come to Him in truth. If we allow the Bible to change our officiating beliefs, then we begin our journey with God living by the truth of the Bible. If we reject truth, then the Bible can't get into us to align us to come into agreement with God and our hearts become harder than ever.

The Revelation of the Bible

Seek ye the LORD while he may be found, call ye upon him while he is near. (Isa. 55:6)

God wants to connect with us through the Bible and He talks to our hearts. The Bible is *a heart knowledge*. We read the Bible to hear God's voice and we respond to Him in our hearts. Desire is not enough. You have to open up to God and invite Him into your heart or you can't understand His book. Until you are alive unto God, how can you possibly understand His ways or His thoughts? God must enliven our darkened spirits. It's like turning on the light before you enter a dark room you've never been in before. How do you know the way until you turn on the light? God has got to get in there and go to work but God is a gentleman and He won't do one thing without your permission. Revelation is a spiritual experience and truth is a spiritual connection with God.

> While it is said, Today if ye will hear his voice, harden not your hearts, as in the provocation. (Heb. 3:15)

All you've got to do is ask and God will respond. God gave us the Bible to serve as an owner's manual for our souls. If we will follow His instructions, the power of God will be released in us so we can experience *life* the way it's meant to be lived. Hearing God's voice is wonderful.

> God, who at various times and in various ways spoke in time past to the fathers by the prophets, Has in these last days spoken unto us by His Son, whom He has appointed heir of all things, through whom also he made the worlds. (Heb. 1:1-2 NKJV)

First God says it (by promise in His Word), then God does it (in demonstrations of historical events) and then God reveals it (by the power of His Spirit) in our hearts. He wants to show us His purpose so we can live. This is what Jesus calls *The Life* in John 14:6. God originally meant for us to live forever in His presence. Jesus' life demonstrates that.

The Law of Revelation

God doesn't just do things. God does everything for a purpose. God never does anything without accomplishing His purpose. In everything God does, He teaches something. God never does anything without teaching something.

In the Bible, God uses earthly things to teach us about heavenly things, natural things to teach us about spiritual things, and visible things to teach us about invisible things. God uses events, people, places, and things in the Old Testament, as types, patterns, figures and examples, to show us things that are going to happen in Christ, which are witnessed in the New Testament. I call God's method of communication the *Secret Language* of the Bible.

The Old Testament is God's credit card and the New Testament is God's debit card. When God promised things in the Old Testament He was putting salvation on a credit card. By making a promise, He was buying salvation they could experience now but would be paid for in the future. In the New Testament, salvation is already paid for on God's debit card. The provision for salvation is already in place so when you call upon God you draw on His goodness that is already paid for. The name of Jesus is the signature and password for everything you have need of whether it's salvation, healing, deliverance or blessing. Jesus will not withhold what He has already purchased for you. Jesus isn't going to make you wait a long time to meet your needs because everything you will ever need is already paid for and it belongs to you. As you exercise your faith and make withdrawals you will see it is the Father's good pleasure to give you the kingdom.

Believers who lived in the Old Testament times *looked forward in faith* by God's promises to see *things to come*. The fathers and the prophets could read events like we watch movies, and see by God's methods the things God was showing them in the natural that would come to pass one day in the spiritual. All those events revealed glimmers of God's original promise in Genesis 3:15, to send the promised seed, His only Son from Heaven, to fulfill His promises. Believers who live in New Testament times, like you and me, *look back in faith* to see the *things that were promised and fulfilled in Christ*. That's the secret to understanding the Bible. Remember, God doesn't just do things, but He does everything for His purpose and in everything He does He teaches something. Only the living God who can walk through time can tell us the future, can be involved in the events of time, and then show us how He accomplished what He promised thousands of years before.

> Now to Him who is able to establish you according to my gospel and the preaching of Jesus Christ, according to the revelation of the mystery kept secret since the world began. (Rom. 16:25 NKJV)

The Bible is God's progressive revelation of Himself, His promises, and the fulfillment of all His promises. We see God began His walk through time with man after creation, sharing His secret with us in the first few chapters of the book of Genesis. God didn't give us His revelation of Himself and His plan of man's redemption all at once, but rather little by little. The Bible begins its revelation to us with the picture of God walking with Adam in the Garden of Eden, which is part of the lesson of the Bible. Eternal life is walking with God forever. However, man fell away from God and began his conquest of a new world order without God. Yet God continued His walk on earth revealing Himself to all those who chose to walk with Him. God purposely doled out bits of information over centuries of time so our enemies in the spirit realm couldn't comprehend God's plan and interfere with His purpose. Those who had the focus of faith could perceive what God did share with humans.

The Old Testament documents the manifestations of God, as He continued to share and expound parts of His secret with those who would walk with Him through time. The Bible says, "*. . . in the fullness of times*," Jesus came from Heaven and told us everything. Then we see God walking with Jesus as the central point of history. Finally, we get to the last book of the Bible, and we see God's secret is fulfilled and His purpose is accomplished. Those who came back to God and walked with God in their lives were blessed and saved. Those who chose not to participate in God's plan were left to their own devices, were destroyed with this present evil world, and perished without God. The Bible reveals the goodness and severity of God (see Rom. 11:22).

> No longer do I call you servants, for a servant does not know what his lord is doing; but I have called you friends, for all things that I have heard of my Father I have made known unto you. (John 15:15 NKJV)

If you can't see God walking through time, then you won't be able to clearly understand the secret of eternity. You'll see the message of the Bible is the same gospel (good news) preached in the New Testament as was preached in the Old Testament. It is the revelation of God's purpose for creation to have an eternal family. The Bible is the good news of the heavenly provision, which a loving God and Father has made through His only Son, to recover man out of the state of death into which he has fallen and to bring him back into the glorious state of life and fellowship, fulfilling His purpose of creation, which is to have a family. Everything began with God's purpose and everything will end with the fulfillment of His purpose. Even today, God is at work accomplishing His purpose for creation and He isn't hindered by the plans of evil men. God communicates with people who love Him. God works through people who walk with Him, and God reveals His secret to His friends.

What God is doing is a secret to His enemies, but it's God's plan to His friends. The world continues with its agenda to build a new world order without God. They tried to do the same thing at Babel because their focus was only upon the creature and the creation, and not the Creator who is blessed, forever. While man's agenda oppresses and manipulates the people, God is at work. While the leaders of the world are busy doing what they think will make the world a better place, though many will be lost, God is fulfilling His purpose and He wants to share His purpose with you.

God Has a Dream

> And to make all men see what is the fellowship of the mystery, which from the beginning of the world hath been hid in God, who created all things by Jesus Christ. (Eph. 3:9)

Through the Bible, God speaks to mankind the same way Martin Luther King Jr. spoke to the leaders of America in his "I Have a Dream" speech, in the late 1960s. Mr. King took a stand and told the leaders of the United States that the Constitution and the Declaration of Independence were the founding documents penned by our forefathers. They proclaim the inalienable right that all men are created equal before God and they guarantee every citizen of the United States the rights of life, liberty, and the pursuit of happiness, regardless of color.

Martin Luther King Jr. said those two documents were like promissory notes to him, but over a century later the citizens of color were still slaves. He said America had written a bad check and he refused to believe the bank of justice had insufficient funds. He drew a line demanding those rights. He said he believed America offered the riches of freedom and the security of justice to all its citizens regardless of color and he had come to cash his check, which the forefathers had written. His dream was that every citizen of color would be given the same rights as all other citizens.

The same way as Martin Luther King Jr. had a dream he gave to America, God has a dream and He gives His "I Have a Dream" speech to us through the Bible. God has given us a written document called the Bible to serve as an anchor for our souls, promising us that He has guaranteed to us the right to live with Him forever, through His Son, Jesus Christ. God's dream was to have and enlarge an eternal family. God created us to be a part of His heavenly family. Before creation God promised you the right to be in His eternal family, but we were carried away by Adam and brought into the bondage of slavery to a world system without God. The Bible calls this world the kingdom of darkness. We can't see God's kingdom, but it is just as real as this see-and-be-seen world. It's like a parallel world in quantum physics.

God created everyone in the human species with the right to have dual citizenship in earth and in Heaven, to be able to walk with Him in paradise forever. Man fell away from God and paradise was lost. Men have been slaves of this kingdom of darkness ever since. God showed us Israel as our example. The people of Israel were the heirs of God's promise but they were in bondage to slavery in Egypt for more than 400 years. God sent Moses to Pharaoh to make His demands to let His people go. This was a historical event in the natural world God used to teach and demonstrate something He has done in the spiritual world for all mankind. God did the same for you and me by Jesus Christ that He did for them through Moses.

God sent His Son from Heaven to destroy Satan's powers of death over mankind, and to demand that he let His people go. Jesus has broken Satan's powers of death over us and the victory is ours. Death need not have the victory over you. Just as the forefathers made provision for every citizen of America, even so God has made provision for every soul born of Adam, regardless of color or culture. God's provision of eternal life belongs to you. It is your inalienable right. This means it is your right whether you are aware of it or not. God has given us eternal life through His Son and God has guaranteed your right to eternal life. With God there is no need for racial justice, social justice or political correctness because His eternal justice, by Jesus Christ, has ensured that spiritual freedom is your right. It is the gift of God. Eternal life is your inheritance and it belongs to you.

> In hope of eternal life, which God, that cannot lie, promised before the world began. (Titus 1:2)

Now I know if someone left you an inheritance you would be quick to claim it. Jesus has left us an inheritance, eternal and more real than a natural inheritance. The New Testament is called "the Last Will and Testament of Jesus Christ." Jesus is the only person who has ever lived, died as a beneficiary, left a will, and rose again to be the executor of His own will. He did that for every human ever born.

Will you investigate what He has left you as an inheritance? Adam walked away from God carrying the whole human race within him, separating us all from God. As a result, we all inherited his spiritually dead nature of living life without God in a degenerated state of sin and death. By God's supernatural power, He has made it possible for us to come back into fellowship with Him so we can truly live. Time is only an opportunity to get ready for eternity. You can walk with God the way Jesus did on earth *if you can believe the words of Jesus.* That is part of the lesson of the Bible.

Jesus is called *the last Adam* in the Bible. Jesus has always walked with God and He didn't leave Heaven and come to earth just to show off. He came to earth to show us eternal life and He died on the cross in our place to give us that life. He took our spiritual death that we might have His eternal life and be able to fellowship with the heavenly Father. It's called the great exchange. He demonstrated to us that eternal life is the lifestyle of walking moment by moment with God. Walking with God forever begins with a response to His invitation. His gift is activated in our hearts when we come to Him. Then we begin our walk with God forever.

Personal Study Notes

CHAPTER 2

THE WORDS *of* GOD

But he answered and said, It is written,
Man shall not live by bread alone, but by every word
that proceedeth out of the mouth of God.

MATT. 4:4

Who's Got the Power?

From God's perspective there are two types of people in the world, the living and the dead. This book will help you determine which one you are. The Bible says, just like our food keeps us alive, even so the words of God make us alive and keep us alive spiritually. Jesus said God's spirit comes through the words of God. Just as God spoke the worlds into existence and everything came to life, even so we come to life spiritually when we hear the words of God. They are the containers that carry God's life and God's spiritual nature. Have you ever heard the phrase, *from God's mouth to my ears?* God wrote His words down so we could hear His voice and see spiritual realities and have fellowship with Him.

> For the word of God is living, and powerful, and sharper than any two-edged sword, piercing even to the division of soul and spirit, and of the joints and marrow, and is a discerner of the thoughts and intents of the heart. And there is no creature hidden from his sight, but all things are naked and open to the eyes of Him to whom we must give an account. (Heb. 4:12-13 NKJV)

The Bible says the words of God are alive and powerful. Notice the dual nature of the words of God. In this passage of scripture we see an inward and outward effect upon the human. In the KJV translation it says God's words are *quick* and powerful. The word quick in the Greek means they are alive. God's words are living things. They give life to the hearer. Then it says they are *sharper than any two-edged sword.* Notice God wants to show us the dual nature, which implies intimate penetration inwardly and outwardly. God's word is a sword of truth with two sides and they are both razor sharp. One side is the death side and the other side is the life side. Then in the KJV it says, *piercing to the dividing asunder of soul and spirit.* So the words of God penetrate into our spirits and souls, which are intimately connected, to help us to understand the difference between what is spiritual and what is soulical. Our spirit is part of our heart. That is the part of us that believes God, loves God and other creatures. Our soul is made up of our minds, our intellects, our wills and emotions. The soul is that part of us that thinks, chooses, learns and feels. The words of God get into our innermost being and affect all our inward parts.

Then it says the words of God *quicken the joints and marrow of the bones.* That means the words of God quicken our mortal bodies. Again notice the intimate nature between the joints and marrow. They are so closely connected that they are one yet separate in nature. The joints represent our outward parts while the marrow represents our inward parts, both interwoven and dependent upon each part. Another scripture says the words of God are life to those that find them and medicine to all their flesh. Finally, it says the words of God *discern the thoughts and intents of the heart.* Our spirits and our souls are so intimately connected together, they are one, yet they are separate in nature. Notice in this scripture that our thoughts are the reflections of our motives. This is as deep as we can go inside ourselves to govern ourselves. Every word of God helps us with that. This is where our nature is formed and determines whether we are wise or foolish. The words of God carry the power of God, yet even God's power is of no power at all unless we believe.

> So then faith cometh by hearing, and hearing by the word of God. (Rom. 10:17)

Notice the double emphasis of our hearing to manifest faith. Every relationship depends upon both sides. The same is true with you and God. The Bible says God is a spirit and He created you to have a relationship with Him but you were separated at birth from your heavenly Father in the Garden of Eden. God wants you to know there is an inheritance laid up in Heaven for you that is incorruptible, undefiled, that will not fade away. Yet the Bible says, *few there will be that will find it.* It isn't just the power of God that makes things happen but it is your response to God's word that consummates your relationship with God and determines your eternal destiny.

> But without faith it is impossible to please him: for he that cometh to God must believe that he is, and that he is a rewarder of them that diligently seek him. (Heb. 11:6)

God has spoken to us but have we heard? God has told us the truth but can we see it? It says *it is impossible to please God without faith.* Pleasing God is the goal of faith. God wants to give you supernatural power in your life but you are the one that turns on the light switch of faith. God is pleased when we hear His words, believe His words and walk with Him in Spirit and in truth by faith.

So then they that are in the flesh cannot please God. (Rom. 8:8)

God is able to manifest Himself to you the way He did with other believers in the Bible, so you can know He is with you, that He loves you and will take care of you. But if you want to walk in the flesh in life and *be your own god*, you will not be able to please God and your relationship with God will be affected. Part of the lesson of the Bible is realizing He is God and we are not.

Can You See?

And the disciples came and said to Him, "Why do You speak to them in parables?" He answered and said to them, "Because it has been given to you to know the mysteries of the kingdom of heaven, but to them it has not been given. For whoever has, to him more will be given, and he will have abundance; but whoever does not have, even what he has will be taken away from him. Therefore I speak to them in parables, because seeing they do not see, and hearing they do not hear, nor do they understand. And in them the prophecy of Isaiah is fulfilled, which says: 'Hearing you will hear and shall not understand, and seeing you will see and not perceive; for the hearts of this people have grown dull. Their ears are hard of hearing, and their eyes they have closed, Lest they should see with their eyes and hear with their ears, Lest they should understand with their hearts and turn, So that I should heal them.' But blessed are your eyes for they see, and your ears for they hear; for assuredly, I say to you that many prophets and righteous men desired to see what you see, and did not see it, and to hear what you hear, and did not hear it." (Matt. 13:10-17 NKJV)

God is at work in the world today. Those who walk in the darkness cannot see what God is doing. They don't even know God is real. They can hear with their ears and see with their eyes, but they do not understand God with their hearts. They can't perceive what God is doing because their hearts haven't become alive unto God by faith. We are spiritually blind by nature because we are operating by a broken program that we have been living by since Adam fell away from God. Every child of Adam has been born with the spiritual tendency to live life without God in spiritual darkness and that is why we die. It isn't your fault or my fault but it is our spiritual condition. We walk in darkness until the light of truth shines into our hearts through the words of God.

The issue between you and God is whether you want to continue to walk in darkness or to come into the glorious light and see God at work in your life. God lets us choose our lifestyle but our own destiny is eternal. The younger we are when we learn the truth, the less there is to unlearn. No matter how successful you become in this world, things will change, but what God is doing is going to remain forever. Wouldn't you like to be a part of what God is doing? Wouldn't you like to be healed of your blindness and see things from the eternal perspective of the Bible? The Bible says, *it has been given unto you to know the mysteries of the Kingdom of Heaven* if you allow God into your heart. Wouldn't you like to know the secret of eternity?

How the Bible Was Written

> For the prophecy came not in old time by the will of man: but holy men of God spoke as they were moved by the Holy Ghost. (2 Pet. 1:21)

The way God wrote the Bible is a good example of how God manifests Himself and how He gets done what He wants done. The Scriptures say God spoke to holy men, which means they were walking with God and loving God. When God spoke to them, these men spoke the words of God they heard to others and those words were written down and meticulously preserved for mankind.

In the Bible we see God intimately spoke to *faith people* who loved Him. God arranged events for *faith people* who walked with Him and He still does today. Many of these people are listed in the eleventh chapter of the book of Hebrews, which is God's Hall of Fame. I call it the Hall of Faith. Even so today God arranges events, circumstances and rewards for people who will come home and walk with Him in faith.

The Bible was written through more than forty different people from all walks of life over a period of about two thousand years. These people were farmers, shepherds, kings, prophets, scholars, slaves, and just ordinary people like you and me, who walked with Him. They believed the promises God had made to the fathers and were living like they were expecting the promises to happen in their lifetime. God manifested Himself unto them because with faith in their hearts, they had ears that could hear Him and eyes that could see Him at work in their lives.

God Never Changes

For I am the LORD, I change not, (Mal. 3:6a)

Jesus Christ the same yesterday, and today, and forever. (Heb. 13:8)

In this world things are changing and people are constantly changing, but God never changes. God is the same yesterday, today, and forever. God walks with us today like He walked with all believers in the Bible. Without faith, we just can't hear Him when He speaks. We can't see Him when He arranges things in our lives. We have ears that do not hear and eyes that cannot see as the scripture says, but He is always present, working to draw you to Himself. The Bible says God is a rewarder of them that diligently seek Him.

God allowed Adam to choose life without God, even though God warned him that life without God is death. Just as Adam walked away from God, even so men walk away from God today. He will let you make the same choice Adam made, even though doing so is a big mistake. There have always been those few who believe God and walk with God and they have experienced His supernatural in their natural lives. As it was with them, even so it is with those few today that walk with God in the truth. God will manifest Himself to you just like He did to them. All things are possible for you if you can believe. The only thing that can separate you from the love of God is you.

But without faith it is impossible to please him: for he that cometh to God must believe that he is, and that he is a rewarder of them that diligently seek him. (Heb. 11:6)

When anyone has faith and walks with God, He will visit them and manifest Himself unto them. Faith takes us into God's presence with hearing ears that can hear His voice. Faith gives us seeing eyes that can see His participation in our lives. With the hearing ears and seeing eyes of faith we develop an understanding heart. That's what turns God on. Just like you get pleasure from walking with your kids, nothing gives God more pleasure than hanging out with His kids. Nothing in this world compares to the glory of hearing God's voice and seeing God's involvement in our life. It is beyond all we can think or imagine. It is the thrill of the heart, the treasure of the soul and it is the secret of eternity.

Where a lot of people miss it is in their understanding of the Bible. They consider it just a historical book of events and people, but the Bible is full of the words of God, which are *alive and powerful*. You can understand the Bible. You don't have to learn *all truth* to understand the Bible. With the right focus, the Bible can become simple to understand. Hopefully, this book helps to give you the focus of faith so faith can come and give you spiritual understanding. It's like an owner's manual for the human spirit. Unless you follow the instructions of the Bible you will never understand the difference between the spirit and the soul.

God wants us to understand Him. God wants to show us what He has done for us and what He will do for you and all your loved ones when you have faith in Him. What He has done for others He will do for you. God never changes. It's our perspective that changes. When we focus on God, we come to see eternal life is living in God's presence, moment by moment, whether in Heaven or on earth. Our faith sees that living life as we walk with God is the same every day, but His mercies are new every morning.

But Wait! There's More

> Every good gift and every perfect gift is from above, and cometh down from the Father of lights, with whom is no variableness, neither shadow of turning. (Jas. 1:17)

Most Bible teachings in our generation are centered on two main Bible doctrines: forgiveness of sins and Heaven when you die. We need to know those things. Without forgiveness of sins we can't go to Heaven. Jesus has paid the price and has made it possible for us to go to Heaven, but Heaven when we die is not the only incentive of the Bible. There is more. There is a whole new world that is yet to come, but there is also a whole new life to live with God on earth. There are those who don't feel comfortable thinking about Heaven because they are satisfied with the kind of life they have on earth. Many feel like the Bible is just a religion, but it isn't. Religion makes empty promises that must be earned by your good works. Religion has gods that don't show up like the historical God of the Bible does. Religion doesn't give eternal gifts like God does.

> The thief cometh not, but for to steal, and to kill, and to destroy: I am come that they might have life, and that they might have it more abundantly. (John 10:10)

The Bible says religion makes the human work for the wages of death. With religion there is no difference if you die in a few years or you die after living 100 years. It is still the same result. You will still go into eternity without God and be separated from Him forever. It is better to never have been born than to live, die, and be lost forever without God. The Bible presents God as the giver of gifts and eternal life through Jesus Christ. His Son is His gift to us. Your very life on earth is the gift of God, and eternal life is the gift of God. How easy to believe is that?

The Bible teaches Jesus came from Heaven to Earth to pay the price for us to be pardoned of sin, to make it possible for us to become citizens of Heaven. As citizens of Heaven, even though we are not perfect, we can walk with God in His power while we're living life on planet Earth. No matter what is taught in the churches, there are those who will be satisfied with just the message of forgiveness of sins and Heaven when we die. Many are satisfied with the traditions of men and entertainment from the pulpit. There will be those who are uncomfortable going to church to hear what they think is religion. The Bible says mere religion is only a form of godliness denying the power of God. I don't like religion either. I like truth and I like seeing the power of God. Many people don't like to hear about Bible subjects such as sin, death and Hell, but these things are real and they affect you forever. How about you? Do you think it is possible there is a greater incentive offered to us in the Bible than just forgiveness of sins and Heaven when you die? I assure you there is more and the Bible calls it *the power of God*.

If You Can Only Believe

Jesus said unto him, if thou canst believe, all things are possible to him that believeth. (Mark 9:23)

The world says, "If you can only imagine." God says, "If you can only believe." What God asks us to believe in the Bible is beyond our imaginations. Let's just imagine you broke the law and did something evil to someone you work with. They could press charges and send you to jail. Then one day you come in to work and this person says, "I forgive you of every evil thing you've ever done." You would probably be relieved you were not going to jail.

Then imagine this person is really a billionaire and he owns an island in the Pacific and he says to you, "In spite of all the things you have done against me, I want to be friends with you and take you out on my yacht and show you the beauty of my island." You'd probably get excited. Well that is kind of what God says He has done for you. He has forgiven all your sins and He has made it possible for you to come to Heaven forever. For the rest of your life God wants to show off His love and goodness toward you.

Now unto him that is able to do exceeding abundantly above all that we ask or think, according to the power that worketh in us. (Eph. 3:20)

But wait. There's more, if you want to be friends with God. Abraham was called the friend of God and God showed off for him. Are you excited now? You should be. The Bible says God has done *exceedingly, abundantly, above* all that you can ask, think or imagine. God has much more in store for you than just forgiveness of sins and Heaven when you die. If you will open up your heart to God, He will show off His goodness to you, and you will be amazed. God is greater than any billionaire and He has a whole new life He wants to show you in the Bible. He has a whole new world He wants to give you for eternity. In this book I want to show you the true incentive of the Bible. I call it the secret of eternity. Don't leave earth without it.

The Heavenly Father

> Call to Me, and I will answer you, and show you great and mighty things, which you do not know. (Jer. 33:3 NKJV)

Every religion ever designed by man or angel presents a god that is impossible to know, but the Bible reveals God to be the heavenly Father. Religion portrays God as a supreme being who is out of reach. Religion tells man what he must do for God but the Bible tells man *what God has done* for him. God wants to show you what He's doing in the Bible and He wants you to be a part of what He's doing. God wants everyone to live forever with Him, and to win in life. God doesn't want anyone to perish. Isn't God good? Yes, God is beyond good.

God leaves the choice up to us. God allowed Adam to walk away from His plan with the whole human race inside him. He will let you walk away from His glorious plan of eternity to be your own god for a moment, but it's a lie. If you think being your own god for a few years on earth is something you have accomplished, you are just deceiving yourself. We have just enough time to figure out how deceived we are and then realize God is giving us the opportunity to put on immortality. No matter what we think we have accomplished, and no matter how well we did with others on earth, it's only for a moment in the timeline of eternity. God has His purpose for creation and He is doing something wonderful that few people will ever realize. In the end, He is the heavenly Father, He is having a family and He loves His kids. Jesus called God His Father and He presented God to us as the heavenly Father. Jesus demonstrated to us that God is love.

By The Words of God

> But he answered and said, it is written, Man shall not live by bread alone, but by every word that proceedeth out of the mouth of God. (Matt. 4:4)

I use a lot of scriptures in this book, but I encourage you to read every word of them and if possible read them out loud. Each scripture is a beam of light shining from Heaven into the darkness of ignorance in our souls. The scriptures are the words that came out of God's mouth. As you read them you will begin to see that when God says the word "life" or "live" He is talking about forever. God's perspective flows out of God's words. They are supernatural and as they enter through your mind into your heart, if you believe, they will release spiritual forces inside you and "quicken you." They will reveal hidden treasures of truth. Don't trick yourself into being bored when you read a scripture. If you read the Bible like an ordinary book of stories you will be bored out of your mind. Man shall not live by bread alone!

If you read the Bible to discover the truth of eternity, God will, as the Bible says, ". . . show you great and mighty things which you know not." You will see God demonstrating spiritual things through historical natural events, showing you *Truth for Eternity*, and you'll be satisfied.

Jesus told the Pharisees, "You know not the scriptures nor the power of God." These people were the doctors of theology in their time and they knew the words of God forwards and backwards, yet they didn't understand God. Their motives were wrong and in their hearts they couldn't see God's focus. Jesus implies we should be able to experience the power of God as we study Scripture.

> My son, attend to my words; incline thine ear unto my sayings. Let them not depart from thine eyes; keep them in the midst of thine heart. For they are life unto those that find them, and health to all their flesh. Keep thy heart with all diligence; for out of it are the issues of life. (Prov. 4:20-23)

Without the power of God in our lives we're just kicking the dirt, shooting at the moon, crowing like a rooster, and running like a mouse on a treadmill. So ponder the scriptures because every one of them is filled with the enlightening and quickening power of God. Every scripture is life to those that find God's words and *health to all their flesh*. In this passage of scripture the word *health* is also translated as *medicine* to all his flesh. God's words are medicine to all your flesh.

I remember one night I was reading a particular scripture out loud and I was trying to understand God's perspective in that scripture. I read the scripture out loud over and over with the purpose of understanding the truth. All of a sudden, I heard God's voice in the scripture and it felt like a jolt of electric force lifted me about an inch off the chair. I was in awe. I realized the awesome power of hearing God's voice in a scripture. I don't remember what the scripture was but I remember the power that jolted me as it exploded inside me. It felt sort of like a shock. I was quickened in my heart by spiritual power that was contained in that scripture.

> It is the spirit that quickeneth; the flesh profiteth nothing: the words that I speak unto you, they are spirit, and they are life. (John 6:63)

The Bible says *God is a Spirit* and *His words are Spirit*, and they quicken the human. What does the word "quicken" mean? In the original Greek it means *to make alive.* The Spirit of God is released into the human by the words of God. Just like my thoughts drop into your mind as I speak words to you, even so the quickening power of God's words fall into our hearts like seeds into the soil. Each truth sprouts up in our hearts and minds and makes us alive unto God. When Jesus says His words are life, He means His divine nature, which we see in Jesus. As your heart embraces the words of God, He quickens you with His Spirit and you become alive unto Him. God says in the Bible, if you will listen unto His words and receive Him, He will give you His life.

The words of God accomplish a dual work in us. They give us life and power. When we hear the words of God, His Spirit quickens us. As His words enter into our ears and fall down into our hearts, they explode with life-giving power inside us. Every word of God shines beams of light and glimmers of truth from Heaven until the eyes of our hearts are opened and we can see truth.

Jesus likened the words of God to seeds that come down into the soil. He said the seeds were the words of God and the soil was our hearts. Some seeds fall upon the stony ground and they have no root in themselves. Some seeds fall into ground with thorns and weeds and they are choked and die. Other seeds fall on dry ground and they wither. Other seeds fall on good ground and they sprout up and bear much fruit. The emphasis is not upon the seeds, but upon the ground. What kind of ground is your heart? Is your heart thorny ground, rocky ground, dry ground, or good ground?

The more we study the Bible and the more God's words penetrate into our hearts, the more we understand God and the more His Spirit quickens us and motivates us to walk with Him. God still speaks to us today in our hearts through the Bible. His words are eternal and will never become worn out by time. God will never tell you anything that does not agree with the Bible.

He Reveals His Secrets to His Friends

The secret of the LORD is with them that fear him; and he will shew them his covenant. (Ps. 25:14)

It is the glory of God to conceal a thing: but the honour of kings is to search out a matter. (Prov. 25:2)

All throughout time God has been talking to holy people who walk with Him. They recorded His words and their experiences in His book as paint strokes in a masterpiece. The Bible is a puzzle that reveals the Glory of God. You can't see the whole picture without putting all of the pieces of the puzzle together. When the whole picture is put together, then you understand what God is showing you. That is how the Bible was written. Each event, each person, each place, in each time, is a lesson of divine expertise, which helps to form the divine masterpiece. It is God's Glory to conceal His secret from unbelievers and to reveal Himself to believers.

God, who at sundry times and in divers manners spake in time past unto the fathers by the prophets, Hath in these last days spoken unto us by his Son, whom he hath appointed heir of all things, by whom also he made the worlds. (Heb.1:1-2)

The Creator created the creature for fellowship with Him. He didn't create us and leave us alone. He's been involved in our world from day one. The human race has been blinded to His presence. Over the centuries of time, God has revealed Himself in many ways, but in these last days He has spoken to us by His Son.

> Henceforth I call you not servants; for the servant knoweth not what his lord doeth: but I have called you friends; for *all things that I have heard of my Father I have made known unto you.* (John 15:15)

Those who respect His Son, God calls His friends, and He is pleased to reveal everything to us. God isn't just all words. He shows up. God is all action. The Bible says God will show us great and mighty things we know not and He will show us things to come. He will guide us into all truth. Before we call unto Him He will answer us. God shows off to His friends. When God shows off, it is wonderful.

Through the Knowledge of God

> My son, if thou wilt receive my words, and hide my command-ments with thee; So that thou incline thine ear unto wisdom, and apply thine heart to understanding; Yea, if thou criest after knowledge, and liftest up thy voice for understanding; If thou seekest her as silver, and searchest for her as for hid treasures; Then shalt thou understand the fear of the LORD, and find the knowledge of God. (Prov. 2:1-5)

That is chewing on the word of God like meat so we can grow up as children of God and share in His divine nature. It says receive His words, hide His commandments, incline your ear, apply your heart, cry out for knowledge, lift up your voice for understanding, seek and search for wisdom as you would search for hid treasures. This passage of scripture describes how to chew on the scriptures until we understand and are able to comprehend the Spirit of Wisdom. He wants to give us wisdom and knowledge and understanding. It comes out of His mouth and into our hearts. He has laid up for us sound wisdom as the target of our faith.

The problem is our hearts. God needs to do some work in your heart to help you see the truth, and He will if you will allow Him to. God says *if* you will do the seeking, *then* you will understand *the fear of the Lord* and find *the knowledge of God* and your heart will be satisfied. You can know that you are safe forever and that you are going to Heaven. You must do the work of seeking and believing in your heart for God's gift to be activated in your spirit that will make you fit for Heaven.

Wisdom Comes to the Wise

> Wisdom is the principal thing; therefore get wisdom: and with all thy getting get understanding. (Prov. 4:7)

Wisdom only comes from God and it comes through the knowledge of God in our hearts and minds. No one person can retain all of God's wisdom but God enlightens all who cry out to Him for wisdom and understanding and it is God's glory to reveal Himself unto us. Wisdom is the principal thing because it is the ability to follow God's instructions and see things from God's eternal perspective. Without God, there is no true wisdom and without God, life is only temporary.

God gives us many words in the Bible so we can digest spiritual things until we are full and can understand God's revelations to us. There are many phrases in the scriptures such as "sound doctrine, a good foundation, the preparation of the gospel of peace, rightly dividing the word of God, that the man of God may be thoroughly furnished unto every good work, etc." that help us clearly realize "man shall not live by bread alone but by every word that comes from the mouth of God." All these phrases imply the fact that "wisdom comes to the wise."

> I am that bread of life. *Your fathers did eat manna in the wilderness, and are dead.* This is the bread which cometh down from heaven, that a man may eat thereof, and not die. (John 6:48-50)

Are you one of the wise? Jesus said He was the Bread of Life that came down from Heaven that a man may eat and not die. He said His words are the words of God that you can chew on like bread and live forever. Let me ask you this, do you chew? If you don't chew and chew on the

Bread of Life you will die. When you eat food do you chew everything just once? If you do you won't live long. Chewing is important for digestion and if you don't chew thoroughly, you won't get the nutrients in your food. As chewing is healthy for the body, so is chewing the word of God for the human spirit and soul. As food is important to the body, even so you must receive the words of God with same importance because the words of God are the food of the human spirit and they bring realignment of the human soul.

Some truths about eternity can't be understood without *many* Scriptures. Some Scriptures explode with several revelations at once. Each Scripture is a container of eternal truth. The more Scriptures you read, the bigger those spiritual containers get. Just like you speak words and I understand what is inside you, even so God's words bring us God's thoughts, God's ways and an understanding of God. However, our understanding of God will take forever to build because God is beyond our imaginations.

God has put in words what He wants to write in our hearts so we can become part of His purpose for creation. Did you know Abraham became a Jew by faith? He is the first human that changed races by believing in God. Abraham is our example. The same thing happens to us when we believe God's words. We change races and receive dual citizenship both in planet Earth and in Heaven.

> He shall cover thee with his feathers, and under his wings shalt thou trust: his truth shall be thy shield and buckler. (Ps. 91:4)

The Bible says He is our buckler as we walk uprightly. Do you know what the "buckler" is? The buckler is a thin layer of armor that fits tightly to the skin of a soldier like the scaly hide of an alligator. As we learn of Him, He begins to enrobe us with Himself to protect us from evil from every angle and all sides. With His help and empowerment, we can keep the paths of judgment, and our way will be preserved as we become true believers. We can understand righteousness, judgment, equity, and every good path.

> Buy the truth, and sell it not; also wisdom, and instruction, and understanding. (Prov. 23:23)

The Bible says we must search for Truth as for hidden treasures and seek wisdom as fine gold, until we understand and find the knowledge of God. Then we will understand God, and be able to walk with God. We become rich spiritually and are able to feel His presence with us always. It is our eternal destiny to walk with God in life and it is our eternal glory to become the children of God.

A prudent man foreseeth the evil, and hideth himself: but the simple pass on, and are punished. (Prov. 22:3)

Throughout the Bible you will find scriptures that separate mankind into two groups: the wise and the fools. The wise man prepares his house for what is coming. Fools just want to have fun. Which group are you in? Are you one of the wise or are you one of the fools? Do you think, "Eat, drink and be merry for tomorrow we die"? Or are you busy looking at the things to come in the Bible and preparing your house? As you learn truth, God will wash your mind and you will be clean of the filthiness of this world. God will cover you with His feathers and you will be amazed at the goodness of God.

And if ye call on the Father, who without respect of persons judgeth according to every man's work, pass the time of your sojourning here in fear. (1 Pet. 1:17)

The goal of this book is to help you understand God's perspective in the Bible and to bring you to the place where you realize the clock of time is ticking and things are winding down for you and all your loved ones. Soon and very soon eternity will begin and you should be ready. There is no need for you to be caught by surprise. You can make yourself ready for eternity. I'm thinking forever; how about you? Before you know it, *poof*, we're gone and eternity has come. And then comes forever.

Are you ready? Do you want to learn the secret of eternity? Let us begin.

Personal Study Notes

CHAPTER 3

PREPARE
Your
HEART

The spirit of man is the candle of the LORD,
searching all the inward parts of the belly.

PROV. 20:27

The Candle of the Lord

Have you been looking for something in life, but don't quite know what it is? What we're looking for is a secret. I call it the secret of eternity. I've written this book about it. Everyone is looking for it, trying to satisfy that hunger and thirst on the inside with outward things. It can't be satisfied with any creature, or creature comforts, or earthly pursuits. You will always have emptiness in your heart until you find God. What we are thirsting for is something that can't be realized with our five senses. It is something supernatural.

> Yea, the light of the wicked shall be put out, and the spark of his fire shall not shine. (Job 18:5)

Inside your heart there is a candle that wants to be lit, and only God can light it. The Bible says your human spirit is the candle of the Lord. Even so your heart is the wick of your candle. Until God lights your wick and sparks your candle, you will never be satisfied. Your candle was created for the love of God. Love can never fully bloom without God because God is love. Loving another creature is not the God kind of love. Loving another person is natural love. Loving God and knowing that God loves you is living life on a supernatural level.

Nothing compares to knowing God and watching God be actively and intimately involved in your life, meeting your needs, and opening your eyes to the realities of eternity. Nothing can satisfy that longing in your heart except God. Your heart was created for God and your heart wants to be loved by God. Your heart will never be secure until you know God loves you. When your candle is finally lit by God and your wick is burning, you will know God loves you, your heart will have peace, and you will be satisfied living life in His presence. With God, your candle shall shine the glory of His love forever.

The Light of Fellowship with God

> That which we have seen and heard declare we unto you, that ye also may have fellowship with us: and truly our fellowship is with the Father, and with his Son Jesus Christ. (1 John 1:3)

The Bible begins in the book of Genesis with God and man walking in fellowship together. It continues with its record of how man's fellowship with God was broken, how death began its dominion over man and how God responded with His promise to make provision for us that fellowship with Him might be restored. The Bible ends in the book of Revelation, with God and man walking in fellowship together for eternity. It was natural for Adam to walk with God in the Garden of Eden. It was natural for Israel to walk with God in the wilderness with God meeting all their needs. Even so we were created for fellowship with God and by the power of God it has been accomplished for us. Even now God wants to be intimately involved in our lives.

> But if we walk in the light, as he is in the light, we have fellowship one with another, and the blood of Jesus Christ his Son cleanseth us from all sin. (1 John 1:7)

The natural human can feel on the inside that he is lost and without God. He doesn't know about God, how to come to God or how to fellowship with God. His heart is looking for God in all the wrong places. All he knows is he can't find what he's looking for.

> Verily, verily, I say unto you, He that heareth my word, and believeth on him that sent me, hath everlasting life, and shall not come into condemnation; but is passed from death unto life. (John 5:24)

The natural man thinks God is dead. God says in the Bible, man is dead. I wonder who is right. I saw a billboard one time that gave me a real chuckle. It said, "God is dead, signed Fred." Then down below that it said, "Fred is dead, signed God." The Bible says, without God man is dead and lost forever. God wrote the Bible to show man he is separated from God and how his separation happened in the beginning. It also shows us how God has made fellowship with Himself possible again through His Son so we can pass from death to life as we come back into fellowship with God again.

When we believe in what God says He has done for us spiritually through Jesus Christ, we pass from death in the natural man and into life in the spiritual man. Being born again of God's spirit, we are able to experience walking with God in the wilderness of this world (like Israel in the Old Testament), trusting God to meet all our needs through Christ in us. God will walk with us the same way He has always walked with His kids. It's part of the secret of eternity. It is His purpose for creation.

With All Your Heart

The fool hath said in his heart, there is no God. (Ps. 14:1)

And ye shall seek me, and find me, when ye shall search for me with all your heart. (Jer. 29:13)

There are those who call themselves atheists and they profess they don't believe in anything. To me that is just a cliché. I don't think it's possible for anyone to believe nothing. Atheism sounds unique, but when it's time to die it produces a fearful heart. The Bible separates all men into two groups: believers and unbelievers; the wise and the fools.

What we truly believe becomes our purpose in life. God has designed us to believe in Him. Yes, it may be true you don't believe in the God of the Bible, but God created your heart to believe. Those who think they believe in nothing are like ships and planes without a compass. Those who believe in nothing are dead while they live. Dead heads produce dead hearts and dead hearts don't belong in Heaven. The truth has to drop down a couple feet from our heads into our hearts. The heart knows better than the head when truth presents itself. When eternity comes you will see truth and you will find out whether you are ready for eternity or not.

The real issue with anyone is, are you satisfied? When you die, will you be satisfied? The Bible says, "The fool has said in his heart there is no God" (Ps. 14:1). You can say in your heart a thousand times there is no God, but that won't change truth. The truth is true whether you know it or not, whether you believe it or not. The truth always has been and always will be the truth. But has *truth* become *reality* for you? If not, then you will never be truly satisfied. The human was designed by God to be satisfied and fulfilled through fellowship with God. There is something on the inside that is gnawing at them and they don't know what it is. I think what they are really saying is, "I haven't found what I am looking for." At least that is an honest statement. At least they are searching.

Have you talked with God in your heart? The Bible says, "Ask, and it shall be given you; seek, and ye shall find; knock, and it shall be opened unto you" (Matt. 7:7). God is the one you are searching for. God knows how to respond to those that seek Him. If you really haven't found what you are looking for and if you will have the courage to come to God with an honest heart, He will reveal Himself to you. He will! For Him to not do so would make either you or Him a liar. The wisdom that is from above comes through the heart of love. Wisdom from God is too high for the fool, but if you will humble yourself, the Bible says God will reward you and reveal Himself to you. You have nothing to lose by calling out and crying out to God for real. It will only save you for eternity. Just because you don't know a secret doesn't mean it isn't real. It just means you don't know it yet. The secret of God is real. It is the secret of eternity.

Come to God

> That they should seek the Lord, if haply they might feel after him, and find him, though he be not far from every one of us. (Acts 17:27)

> He shall call upon me, and I will answer him: I will be with him in trouble; I will deliver him, and honour him. (Ps. 91:15)

When God reveals Himself to you, you will know it. There will be no doubt. It will be obvious in a hundred different ways. When God introduces Himself to you, it will be at the perfect time and you will know God has done something supernatural in you. When you call out and cry out to God with all your heart, the Bible says He will answer you.

It's like meeting your spouse for the first time. First there are the sweaty palms, and then there is the beating heart, then the racing thoughts of the mind, and then comes contact. The same is true with God. He will not come down and do a dance in front of you, and God isn't going to put on a show or perform something for you that He won't do for someone else.

Entertainment is not enlightenment. God loves you as much as He loves anyone else and God loves others as much as He loves you. Just as relationships work with humans, so it is with God. First words are spoken, then actions happen, then there is contact, and love blooms. God is the answer your heart is looking for and it pleases God to respond to your heart. The overwhelming force of God's response to you is love. God responds to love. The Bible says God is love. God has made provision for you and it pleases Him to set your heart on fire and give you the thing you are looking for, which is God's love. The name of Jesus is the key that unlocks God's love towards you.

The Right Way

> Fear not, little flock; for it is your Father's good pleasure to give you the kingdom. (Luke 12:32)

The Bible says love is the royal law of God's kingdom. Imagine a world where love is the only law. God wants to share His secret with everyone. But God only shares His secret with those that love Him and who walk in His love. It is God's pleasure to have fellowship with us but relationship comes before fellowship. That's why we were created for love. Knowing God is eternal life and eternal life is the gift of God's love. Humans can't handle the truth without being made ready for it. We can't walk with God the way we are. Our nature is wrong. We can hardly believe God truly loves us without God making it clear to us. We can hear it a thousand times and still find it almost impossible to believe God loves us, but the moment we do, God's supernatural power is activated in our hearts and all things become new.

> For when *we were yet without strength*, in due time *Christ died for the ungodly*. For scarcely for a righteous man will one die: yet peradventure for a good man some would even dare to die. But God commendeth his love toward us, in that, *while we were yet sinners, Christ died for us*. Much more then, being now justified by his blood, we shall be saved from wrath through him. For if, *when we were enemies,*

we were reconciled to God by the death of his Son, much more, being reconciled, we shall be saved by his life. (Rom. 5:6-10)

The Bible says God demonstrated His love for us while we were yet sinners, enemies of God and without strength. It says Jesus died for the ungodly. That includes you and me. While they were nailing the nails into His hands and feet, Jesus was saying, "God forgive them for they know not what they do." The love of God through Jesus has been historically demonstrated to us. How we respond to God's love determines our eternal destiny.

The Good News of the Bible is, we can come to God and God can change our hearts and make us right. If we want to continue to live life being our own gods, we will never come to God the right way. He requires that we humble our hearts and recognize that He is God and we are not. Heaven is God's home and rebels aren't allowed in. The world calls it protocol. If the President invites me to the White House, I have the right to visit with the President, but I still can't go in just any way I want. I can only go into the White House the right way. There are rules I must obey and protocols I must follow before I can enter the White House. If I won't follow the rules, I won't be allowed in. The same is true with God. We can only come to God His way.

Until the human is made ready, he cannot come to God. He hungers and thirsts for God because his heart knows that is what he was created for, but we can't understand God just with our heads. We can only understand God with our hearts and that changes the way we think in our minds. Many believers can go for years without real change until what is in their heads drops down into their hearts and becomes true faith. When we come to Him with all our hearts, He reveals Himself to us by His Spirit inside our hearts. God reveals Himself and His secret to our hearts, and then it makes sense to our minds. Our minds alone can't handle the truth of God.

For whoso findeth me findeth life, and shall obtain favour of the LORD. But he that sinneth against me wrongeth his own soul: all they that hate me love death. (Prov. 8:36)

God is calling out to you in three ways: body, soul and spirit. God has met all your needs, spirit, soul and body. Will you respond to His invitation?

God has done His part. It's like a marriage. One person says to the other, "Will you marry me?" The one person has done his part and he is now marry-able, but the other person must respond or the marriage isn't possible. God has already responded to you before you were born. God came down from Heaven in Christ and opened the door of His fellowship of love. Before you asked He answered. Before you sought Him He was already there.

> And I say unto you, Ask, and it shall be given you; seek, and ye shall find; knock, and it shall be opened unto you. (Luke 11:9)

Have you truly sought God yet? Have you knocked on the door and asked God to have fellowship with you yet? If not, what's holding you back? God says those who call on Him are wise and those who refuse to call upon Him are fools. The Bible says all they that hate Him love death.

The Wisdom of God

> Hast thou heard the secret of God? and dost thou restrain wisdom to thyself? (Job 15:8)

The wisdom of God in the Bible tells us how to get our candles lit by God. Until then it is a mystery and a secret. Until God turns on the light, truth is the hidden wisdom. Everything Jesus taught centered on the human receiving eternal life from God. The supernatural power that comes from Heaven is not found in any mere religion. God is real. Heaven is real. The wisdom of God is real. You can almost find as many books that promise a higher wisdom as there are deceptions, but the Bible reveals God's hidden wisdom. Jesus said the Bible gives us true wisdom that leads to eternal life. Jesus' resurrection was a historical event that proved the wisdom of His words was the truth.

> Such knowledge is too wonderful for me; it is high; I cannot attain unto it. (Ps. 139:6)

Religions created by men or angels promise a higher wisdom, but they don't satisfy. The Bible tells us even Satan himself masquerades as an angel of light. The only power that religions have is deception. They do not deliver anyone from death; so what good are they?

> For such are false apostles, deceitful workers, transforming themselves into the apostles of Christ. And no marvel; for Satan himself is transformed into an angel of light. Therefore, it is no great thing if his ministers also be transformed as the ministers of righteousness; whose end shall be according to their works. (2 Cor. 11:13-15)

How can you tell when a deception is a deception if you are deceived by it and think it's the truth? If you knew the answer to that you wouldn't be deceived, right? Hitler killed over six million Jews and many others and thought he was right, but he was deceived. There are those that think like that today and believe they are right. There are even some lies that are supernatural. Killing people in the name of religion is a supernatural lie. Just because something is supernatural doesn't make it God. Yes, there are demon powers that masquerade as angels sent from God to deceive men, but just because there is some sort of supernatural manifestation doesn't mean it is God.

Look at what happened with Adam and Eve. They fell away from God because they chose to believe an agenda campaigned by the fallen angel Satan, but it was a lie. Their actions supernaturally brought the curse of death into the human race. They chose to embrace the agenda of a fallen angel rather than believe the words of God. The goal of religions created by fallen angels is to provide belief systems that men can focus their faith in that will separate man from God, and bring death and destruction to God's creation. The goal of the Bible and the focus of all Jesus' teachings are to bring us back unto God forever. Through studying the Bible and walking with God, you can come to know the secret of eternity. It will surprise you, enlighten you, change you, empower you, and quicken you.

It's a Mystery

> But we speak *the wisdom of God* in a mystery, even *the hidden wisdom*, which God ordained before the world unto our glory. (1 Cor. 2:7)

Imagine Jesus coming to Earth from a far and distant place called Heaven to give us such good news that it is beyond description. The secret of eternity is wonderful news. It's the *mystery of God* and the *wisdom of God*. God wants to show it to you. Then it will no longer be a secret, but it will be the joy and glory of your heart, and you will be turned into a new man.

> And to make all men see what is the fellowship of *the mystery*, which from the beginning of the world hath been *hid in God*, who created all things by Jesus Christ. (Eph. 3:9)

God wrote the Bible to help every human understand what He is doing in earth. Many people read and study the Bible without really understanding it. Yes, we can understand Bible concepts but still fail to understand God's purpose, which is the theme of the Bible. When you first meet someone, you can understand their words but you still don't know what's in their heart for a while. You have to get to know them first. The same is true with God also. The Bible is a supernatural book, written by a supernatural person, called the living God, to reveal the *Truth of Eternity* to us. We can't see God, but God is more real than what we can see. God wants to reveal Himself to us so we can know Him and His purpose. God doesn't just want to tell us about Himself. He wants to have a relationship with you. That is why He created you and that is why you exist.

The Shield of Darkness

> But he that hateth his brother is in darkness, and walketh in darkness, and knoweth not whither he goeth, because that darkness hath blinded his eyes. (1 John 2:11)

Jesus said, "Thy word is truth." He said, "Man shall not live by bread alone, but by every word that comes from the mouth of God." The deceptions of this world, which have trained you to live separate from God, have become the blinders that are upon the eyes of your heart and mind. Layers upon layers of deception have been built up over thousands of years. They have forged the ancient shield of darkness that covers our minds. Every lie we believe, and every lust that manipulates us in our lives blocks the light of God and blinds us to the *Truth of Eternity*. A new layer of darkness is formed upon that shield with every generation of man. Only the words of God can penetrate Satan's shield of darkness that blinds the minds of men to the truth.

> In whom *the god of this world hath blinded the minds* of them, which believe not, lest the light of the glorious gospel of Christ, who is the image of God, should shine unto them. (2 Cor. 4:4)

Just like seeds go down into the ground, and just like sperm penetrates the egg in the womb, even so God's words come down from Heaven and penetrate that ancient shield of darkness until each seed pierces through and begins to explode with revelation in our hearts, to open our eyes to the *Truth of Eternity*. Every word of God acts like a drop of acid upon that shield of darkness, causing another layer to dissolve until the light can shine in and we can see truth. Today, God gladly and openly reveals His secret by His Holy Spirit to those whose hearts are ready to receive it. We begin to realize we are eternal beings. We begin to see we are spiritually dead without God. We see our soul is in danger of being lost. The light of the glorious gospel of Christ is shining in our hearts so we can come to know Him.

The Great Lie

> And no marvel; for Satan himself is transformed into an angel of light. (2 Cor. 11:14)

The Bible talks a lot about Satan. The more you know about him and his operation in earth, the better you will be able to protect yourself from his ability to cause destruction. People are searching everywhere all the time for that thing inside their heart that only God can satisfy. They don't realize they are looking for God, so they look in all the wrong places. They wind up deceived because Satan offers us an unlimited amount of knowledge, devices, lusts, and pursuits, which help us to be our own gods and promise satisfaction. But the heart cries, "I can't get no satisfaction." Nothing in this see-and-be-seen world can satisfy the heart because God created us for fellowship with Him. That part of us inside our heart is designed only for God and He alone can bring peace and remove from us the fear of death.

> Let no man beguile you of your reward in a voluntary humility and worshipping of angels, intruding into those things, which he hath not seen, vainly puffed up by his fleshly mind. (Col. 2:18)

Satan is real and he is your enemy. He is the original terrorist. He tricked the world into believing life can be beautiful without God and death is just a fallacy. But the devil is a liar and the Bible teaches that Satan has deceived the whole world. Jesus called him a liar, a thief, a murderer and a robber. Deception is the devil's specialty. Satan's job is to hide the truth of the Bible from the human and he does his job very well. We need God's help just to be able to see the *Truth of Eternity*. God wrote the Bible to show us how He has delivered us from Satan's power through Jesus Christ.

> And the great dragon was cast out, that old serpent, called the Devil, and Satan, which deceiveth the whole world: he was cast out into the earth, and his angels were cast out with him. (Rev. 12:9)

There is coming a day when Satan will be cast out of planet Earth, but until then it is Satan's agenda to rule a world system without God. Satan's promise to us, that you can be your own god, is the foundation of his kingdom. That is the *Great Lie*. Just as Satan deceived Eve in the Garden of Eden, even so he has deceived the whole world. The Bible wants you to know that from the very beginning, Satan started your separation from God. However, God is finishing the situation through His only Son. Jesus has come from Heaven to tell us the truth and He has broken Satan's powers of death over us. In the meantime, multitudes of people remain deceived *by the god of this world*. Every man-made or angelic-made religion, and every solution other than the Bible, allows the human to use that particular belief system and still retain Satan's be-your-own-god philosophy. Every lie of religion is built upon the cornerstone of that one great lie of "you can be your own god." The Bible doesn't let humans be their own gods. The Bible makes the human come to the true God without the godhood of self, because the self is a great enemy to both God and man. Selfish angels and selfish humans, who want to be their own gods, will be satisfied but for a moment in eternity, and then the day of their separation from God becomes permanent and the truth becomes evident.

> Remember the former things of old: for I am God, and there is none else; I am God, and there is none like me, declaring the end from the beginning, and from ancient times the things that are not yet done, saying, My counsel shall stand, and I will do all my pleasure. (Isa. 46:9-10)

Hath Blinded Our Minds

> But if our gospel be hid, it is hid to them that are lost: In whom the god of this world hath blinded the minds of them which believe not, lest the light of the glorious gospel of Christ, who is the image of God, should shine unto them. (2 Cor. 4:3-4)

Again, I want to repeat to you that the Bible says the god of this world, Satan, has blinded our minds to the *Truth of Eternity* and the only thing that can remove the darkness within our hearts is the light of truth. It is human nature to live life without God. It is Satan's self program that has taught us to be our own gods. That program has blinded our minds from the truth. We think we can be our own gods and live life without God, trying to satisfy our inward longings with outward things. That is not how God created us.

> For God, who commanded the light to shine out of darkness, hath shined in our hearts, to give the light of the knowledge of the glory of God in the face of Jesus Christ. (2 Cor. 4:6)

The human heart doesn't want to die. That thing inside your heart knows that without God you won't make it and all will be lost. We can't even see the deceptions within our hearts and minds without God's help. We cannot deliver ourselves from the ways of self the world has trained us to walk in. The supernatural power that will deliver us from evil must come from God.

That's why Jesus came to earth. God historically sent His Son to tell us the truth and to show us the life and then Jesus died on the cross to give us the life.

> While we look not at the things, which are seen, but at the things, which are not seen: for the things which are seen are temporal; but the things which are not seen are eternal. (2 Cor. 4:18)

God Reveals Truth by His Spirit

> Now to him that is of power to stablish you according to my gospel, and the preaching of Jesus Christ, according to *the revelation of the mystery*, which was *kept secret* since the world began . . . (Rom. 16:25)

Philosophy reveals nothing, but it's entertaining. Proverbs 18:2 says, "A fool hath no delight in understanding, but that his heart may discover itself." Philosophy will ask simple questions such as, who am I, why am I here, and what is my purpose? Duh! God is the only one who can answer all your questions and He does so through the Bible. Religion will provide men with belief systems that make promises, which can never be realized by the greatest achievers, and cannot bring peace to your soul.

> Whereby, when ye read, ye may understand my knowledge in the mystery of Christ, which in other ages was not made known unto the sons of men, as it is now revealed unto his holy apostles and prophets by the Spirit. (Eph. 3:4-5)

In the day of death, you will not fear because you know truth. Nothing else satisfies. Don't put it off, because we are not promised tomorrow. God wants to show you things that will change your life.

> Even the mystery, which *hath been hid* from ages and from generations, but now is *made manifest* to his saints. (Col. 1:26)

The Bible says God wants to show you His secret. It was kept a secret for thousands of years, but He is now revealing everything to us. He wants to make it manifest in our hearts so we can get ready for Heaven. If you haven't found what you are looking for, then take a look at the secret of eternity and see if you are satisfied. God will reveal everything to you by His Spirit if you ask Him to. He loves you and wants you to know the truth of eternity.

The Truth Will Make You Free

Then said Jesus to those Jews which believed on him, *if ye continue in my word, then are ye my disciples indeed; And ye shall know the truth, and the truth shall make you free.* (John 8:31-32)

Jesus only spoke the truth. Jesus said to His disciples, "if you continue *in* my word you will know the truth and the truth will make you free." That word *in* means more than just listening to His words. It means you are so full of His words that they are *in* you and you are *in* them. Notice this passage of scripture doesn't say the truth shall *set you free*. It says, if you continue in my word you will *know the truth* and the truth will *make you free*. That's the system that leads to freedom.

- ✔ Continue in my Words
- ✔ You will know the Truth
- ✔ The Truth will make you free

Jesus said, "When you know the Truth it will make you free." Truth will contradict the facts. Just because something is a fact doesn't make it the truth. Facts will change. Truth is true forever. Truth is the knowledge of eternity. Just because you don't know truth yet doesn't stop it from being true. It just stops being true for you. When truth becomes reality for you, then the truth will make you free. The phrase, *make you free*, implies a hard working process of growth and maturity that causes you to become free as you continue. Free from what? Free from the Curse of poverty, sickness and death.

Christ hath redeemed us from the curse of the law, being made a curse for us: for it is written, Cursed is every one that hangeth on a tree. (Gal. 3:13)

Free from spiritual blindness

But if our gospel be hid, it is hid to them that are lost: In whom *the god of this world hath blinded the minds* of them which believe not, lest the light of the glorious gospel of Christ, who is the image of God, should shine unto them. (2 Cor. 4:3-4)

Free from bondage to corruption

Because the creature itself also shall be delivered from the bondage of corruption into the glorious liberty of the children of God. (Rom. 8:21)

Free from the Law of Sin and Death

For the law of the Spirit of life in Christ Jesus hath made me free from the law of sin and death. (Rom. 8:2)

Free from the Wicked One

We know that whosoever is born of God sinneth not; but he that is begotten of God keepeth himself, and that wicked one toucheth him not. And we know that we are of God, and *the whole world lieth in wickedness.* (1 John 5:18,19)

Free from Sin

But now being made *free from sin*, and become servants to God, ye have your fruit unto holiness, and the end everlasting life. (Rom. 6:22)

Free from the World System

And you hath he quickened, who *were dead in trespasses and sins*; Wherein in time past ye *walked according to the course of this world*, according to the prince of the power of the air, *the spirit that now worketh in the children of disobedience* among whom also we all had our conversation in times past in the lusts of our flesh, fulfilling the desires of the flesh and of the mind; and were *by nature the children of wrath,* even as others. (Eph. 2:1-3)

Jesus Promises Us an Endless List of Freedoms

If the Son therefore shall make you free, ye shall be free indeed. (John 8:36)

I've listed only a few scriptures above that talk about how the Son of God makes us free and from what things we are made free. Everyone thinks they are unique and uniquely free to be themselves and they are not like anybody else, but the Bible says we are all under the same curse, we all have the same human nature of life without God and we all have the same eternal destiny and only God can make us free.

God is a Spirit and they that worship him must worship him in spirit and in truth. (John 4:21-24)

Learning truth from the Bible is coming to know God. Revealing the truth of eternity to us is one of the greatest manifestations of God's love. Knowing the truth of eternity will make you free from ignorance, deception, lust, mediocrity, and free from the fear of death, free from the earthly nature of living for self and nobody else. The kind of freedom Jesus is talking about isn't freedom from just a few faults and sins. The kind of freedom the Bible is talking about only comes through the knowledge of the truth. We will be free from the controlling powers of all the deceptions this world trains us to believe in, so we will feel comfortable living life without God. Your freedom, which God has provided, can only come by the words of Jesus Christ. What percentage of freedom are you walking in?

Pilate therefore said unto him, Art thou a king then? Jesus answered, thou sayest that I am a king. *To this end was I born, and for this cause came I into the world, that I should bear witness unto the truth.* Every one that is of the truth heareth my voice. Pilate saith unto him, *what is truth*? And when he had said this, he went out again unto the Jews, and saith unto them, I find in him no fault at all. (John 18:37, 38)

Jesus said He came from Heaven to earth to tell us the truth. If you are truly searching for the truth you will be able to hear His voice. Your knowledge of the truth for eternity will change you as a person. You will have the eternal perspective, free from the limitations of this world. You will be able to understand the Bible and walk in fellowship with the unseen God. The secret of eternity is a knowledge that belongs to every human being and it is activated the moment we believe. It is the gift of God and it lasts forever.

It is easy to see in our present world, therefore it is safe to say there is a problem that man cannot solve and it requires a supernatural solution that only God can provide. In this next chapter we will discuss the human problem and after that we will go into God's solution for the human problem. Then you will better understand your need to be made free from your bondage to this world so you can be made ready for eternity in God's world. Will you let truth *make* you free?

Personal Study Notes

CHAPTER 4

HUMAN, *You* HAVE A PROBLEM

And as it is appointed unto men once to die,
but after this the judgment.

HEB. 9:27

The Death Problem

When Adam and Eve submitted to Satan, they gave him their *God-given dominion* over the planet and their spiritual nature changed. God didn't look down from Heaven and say, "It's a good thing those evil humans are doomed." No, God immediately got involved. He has been involved with our messy problem from the very moment it began. God immediately made us a promise.

> And I will put enmity between thee and the woman, and between thy seed and her seed; it shall bruise thy head, and thou shalt bruise his heel. (Genesis 3:15)

God wasn't caught off-guard. God knew what would happen. He immediately promised Adam and Eve a solution. The Bible is that historical document that shows us how man's death problem began and how God has provided His solution, which delivers us from the power of death. Before we get into the solution, let's talk more about the problem. As a child of Adam, you are affected by the problem. The better you understand the human problem from God's perspective, the more you will marvel at God's solution.

You can divide the truth of the Bible into two categories: death and life. Those are the two trees that were in the midst of the Garden of Eden. That is part of the lesson of the Bible. These two words, death and life, properly understood, are the keys that unlock all the truths of the Bible.

So what is the problem? We can call it evil, lust, adultery, greed, murder, selfishness, poverty, sickness, disease, and so on. The problem is death. Until we understand the death problem we will never understand God's solution. The Bible is about a human problem, which the human cannot solve, that requires a supernatural solution, which only God can provide. God is the only one that can fix the death problem in planet Earth. That is what the Bible is all about. The Bible sums up the whole lifestyle of living without God into one word: death. Every problem on earth is rooted in death. Sickness and disease can be described as limited or premature death because it is trying to kill you. However, the reality of death is simply separation from God.

We can say that death is the lifestyle of living life without God. When the creature is separated from the Creator, he is dead. He is without the life of God and his life is a lifestyle of living without God. That is why we die. Life without God is *spiritual death*, and that is why we experience physical death. The problem is death and God's solution for the problem, believe it or not, is life. However, the life solution doesn't work the way the natural mind supposes. It works by the Spirit of God. The resurrection of Jesus proves this. God provided the Scriptures for us to make it easier for us to understand the nature of death. We humans think from the mindset of life and death. The truth of the Bible is understood in the framework of death and life, and *not* life and death. When we can see God's perspective, our deceptions will begin to go away. We must see truth as reality before it's too late. We tend to read the Bible from the human perspective and when we do, we see a bunch of Bible stories. God wants to teach us what death is and what life is.

The Bible teaches lessons of eternity and nothing will change in our hearts until we see God's perspective. We are no match for death, but death is no match for God. As the Creator, God has done a masterful job of creating us, and as the heavenly Father, God has done an excellent job of making provision for us so we can live and not die. You ask, if we're all going to die, then what do I mean God wants us to live and not die? Death isn't what we think it is and neither is life. There is a deception to death. We have all been deceived by it and God wants to open our eyes to the truth.

> But she that liveth in pleasure is dead while she liveth.
> (1 Tim. 5:6)

We think we are alive and are going to die, but the truth is we are dead, we are going to die, and after death we are going to be judged. From God's perspective, we are already dead. We were born dead. That is why we die. God wants to make us alive so we can live. Death isn't just the human being separated from the physical body. Death is a way of life that ends in death. Death is the reason we die. God sent Jesus to destroy death for us so we could live because God wants us to live and not die. Later on in this chapter I discuss the three levels of death.

Thou Shalt Surely Die

> But of the tree of the knowledge of good and evil, thou shalt not eat of it: for *in the day* that thou eatest thereof thou shalt *surely die*. (Genesis 2:17)

In the Bible, the first thing God brought up with Adam was the subject of death. God warned Adam about death. Adam failed to follow God's instructions. That is also part of the lesson of the Bible, and it is the same issue for every human. No matter what voices you may hear, it is always better to follow God's instructions and live. Adam's disrespect towards God's instructions brought the creation under the dominion of death. God instructed Adam, saying, "Don't eat of that tree." Adam and Eve ate of the forbidden fruit, of the forbidden tree, and we can clearly see death has had dominion over the human race ever since, yet God had nothing to do with it. Death originated with Satan. Death was never a part of God's original plan. Death is an enemy of God and man. Death is the human problem only God can solve. Death is part of the curse that was activated on the earth when Adam and Eve rebelled against God's plan and purpose. An accurate understanding of death can be found in God's first mention of it in the Bible. The first thing God wants to do in the Bible is tell us what death is.

Let's focus on the two phrases I've underlined in the scripture, which are "in the day" and "surely die." God told Adam, *In the day* you eat of the Tree of Knowledge of Good and Evil, you shall *surely die.*" The phrase *in the day* means *that very day,* so there is an immediate effect that happens when we walk away from God. This phrase *"surely die"* is the Hebrew word *mut,* which is pronounced *"mooth."* This Hebrew word is used twice in this scripture as "you shall mut mut" and is translated as "surely die." It's a plural word, meaning multiple deaths, and can be translated in the Hebrew as "you shall die, die," or "in dying you shall die." This plural Hebrew word for deaths, pronounced in this passage of scripture here as "surely die," is saying to us that death is a plural process. Death isn't just the body dying. Man is made up of three parts: spirit, soul, and body. Death is experienced on three levels. Death affects our spirit, soul, and body, in that order. Satan said to them, "You won't surely die, for in the

day that you eat God knows you will be like gods knowing good and evil."
The truth is, Satan lied.

> And the serpent said unto the woman, Ye shall not *surely die*:
> For God doth know that *in the day* ye eat thereof, then your eyes
> shall be opened, and ye shall be as gods, knowing good and evil.
> (Genesis 3:4-5)

The first lie Satan told Adam and Eve was, you won't "surely die."
Whatever you hear that contradicts God's word has death in it because the
Bible says in Hebrews 6:18, "It is impossible for God to lie, and God is not
a man (or angel) that He should lie." If you are going to believe something,
believe what God says. Make sure the thing you believe isn't a lie. In the
day of death, ignorance is no excuse. The second lie Satan was implying
to Adam and Eve is, "you can be your own gods." Knowing good and evil
doesn't make us as gods. Knowledge alone doesn't make us as gods. We have
more knowledge in the world today than ever before, yet man is more corrupt than ever before and he is still dying every day. Quantity of knowledge
isn't as important as the quality of knowledge. Knowledge that includes
God produces life. If your knowledge leaves God out, it is dead knowledge
and it is limited to knowing only good and evil. If you live by that knowledge, it makes you spiritually dead and separated from God. Like a tree
that produces no fruit but has pretty green leaves, knowledge without God
produces nothing of eternal value. Knowledge without God is deceptive and
Satan is the master of deception, but the Truth shall make you free.

> Because that, when they knew God, they glorified him not as God,
> neither were thankful; but became vain in their imaginations, and
> their foolish heart was darkened. Professing themselves to be wise,
> they became fools, and changed the glory of the incorruptible God
> into an image made like to corruptible man, and to birds, and to
> four-footed beasts, and creeping things. Wherefore God also gave
> them up to uncleanness through the lusts of their own hearts, to
> dishonour their own bodies between themselves: Who changed the
> truth of God into a lie, and worshipped and served the creature more
> than the Creator, who is blessed forever. Amen. (Rom. 1:21-25)

When Adam and Eve obeyed Satan, they came under Satan's curse, and they died unto God. Their spiritual nature changed. They died spiritually the moment they ate and they began to die physically. They were born of Satan's "be your own god and live life without God philosophy." They became unfruitful for the Kingdom of God. It says their eyes were opened and they knew they were naked and were afraid. This means they knew the moment they ate that they became children of the devil and were *alienated from the life of God*. The light of the glory of knowing God went out. That is when Satan became the god of this world, the Bible says. The moment they spiritually died, we all spiritually died because every human being ever born was in Adam's loins when he spiritually died. Their spiritually dead nature passed on to the whole race. By them not respecting the words of their Creator, Satan captured the whole human race with a lie, and all of creation came under a curse. As a result, God's creation doesn't continue to work according to God's original design. This was the first battle ever fought. Another created being, a fallen angel called Satan, highjacked God's creature, man and woman, got them under his control and separated the creation from the Creator.

The whole world now lives by the satanic principle of living life without God, but life without God is spiritual death and that is why we die. Death is a way of life that ends in death. *Death and Life is the message of the Bible*. No religion provides the solution to our death problem. History bears witness to this fact. The moment they sinned against God, man's life became the lifestyle of death, serving the creature rather than the Creator who is blessed forever. That very day they died unto God, and when they died spiritually, they began to die physically. The Bible wants us to understand that any creature that is separated from the Creator is dead spiritually and that is why he eventually dies physically. When Adam and Eve walked away from God and jumped on Satan's bandwagon, death began its reign over man, and death has reigned over man ever since.

> For the wages of sin is death; but the gift of God is eternal life through Jesus Christ our Lord. (Rom. 6:23)

Notice the contrast of the phrases *the wages of sin* and *the gift of God* in this scripture. The phrase "the wages of sin" sounds like you are working for a boss who pays wages and the Bible says that's exactly what we are doing. We now work in a world system that functions without God. We get paid to promote the world system and to buy into its agenda. What do we earn? Spiritual death. The deception is, we get to experience what it is like to be our own gods and live life without God for a few years; but the truth is, it's only a moment in eternity.

> But if our gospel be hid, it is hid to them that are lost: In whom *the god of this world hath blinded the minds* of them which believe not, lest the light of the glorious gospel of Christ, who is the image of God, should shine unto them. (2 Cor. 4:3,4)

The Bible calls Satan the god of this world. It represents him as the spiritual taskmaster, working to build a world system without God, and with his whip he oppresses mankind like Pharaoh oppressed the children of Israel. He rewards every human with the wages of death. He cracks that whip and then we die. Death is a law for every child of Adam in this world. Yet the Bible says *the gift of God is eternal life*. Do you see the contrast between the wages of sin, something you work for, and the gift of God, something that is freely given?

> For the law of the Spirit of life in Christ Jesus hath made me free from the law of sin and death. (Rom. 8:2)

When Adam sinned, he initiated a Law of Sin and Death in his spirit, which was passed on to every human within his loins. It is our inheritance. This passage of scripture is talking about a law that cannot be changed, except by a higher law. The Law of Sin and Death is the "be your own god" focus of self. The only law that is higher than the Law of Sin and Death is the law of the Spirit of Life in Christ Jesus. The divine nature of Christ, God calls Life. His divine nature lives for God and is the only spiritual nature that can free us from the law of sin and death. From God's perspective, those are the two laws of the universe: death and life. The only reason we say "life and death" is because mankind has been deceived by the devil into thinking he is alive and not dead. But the lesson of the Bible is, *life without God* is death. That is why we die.

The Three Levels of Death

> And the very God of peace sanctify you wholly; and I pray God your whole spirit and soul and body be preserved blameless unto the coming of our Lord Jesus Christ. (1 Thess. 5:23)

What is death? Simply put, death is separation from God. If you are separated from God, you are dead. There are three manifestations of death. They are spirit, soul and body and God wants to save us spirit, soul and body. These are the three levels of death.

- ✔ **Spiritual Death**   Separation from God
- ✔ **Physical Death**   Separation from the body
- ✔ **Eternal Death**   Separation from God forever

The Bible says the human race was separated from the heavenly Father at birth. Imagine the father who has a child only to watch it die. Imagine how God felt when He saw Adam die. Imagine how God felt when He saw that in Adam we all died and were separated from God. That's how every human is born. We experienced everything that Adam experienced when he sinned, his judgment, his separation from God, his condemnation and his spiritual nature of death while he lives. It is our inheritance from our progenitor. Thank God He didn't abort us. God gave us all the right to live and move and have our being even if we choose death. But the good news is, God is able to make us alive again.

> In this the *children of God* are manifest, and the *children of the devil*: whosoever doeth not righteousness is not of God, neither he that loveth not his brother. (1 John 3:10)

When Adam bowed the knee to Satan in the Garden, Adam's *God-given dominion* over creation was transferred to Satan who became *the god of this world,* the Bible says. It was a legal transaction. Adam became a child of the one whom he obeyed. The nature of the creature is known by its ways. When Adam became a child of the devil, we all became children of the devil. So the Bible says in 1 Corinthians 15:22, ". . . in Adam all die."

We all have Adam's spiritual nature and therefore we are spiritually dead. Because we are all spiritually dead we all die physically. If we are all spiritually dead, when we die physically we will remain eternally dead.

> Know ye not, that to whom ye yield yourselves servants to obey, *his servants ye are to whom ye obey*; whether of sin unto death, or of obedience unto righteousness? (Rom. 6:16)

To simply summarize the problem of every human's life, I'll say it again. Everyone born of Adam is born separated from God. Being separated from God causes us to be separated from our physical bodies at death. If we are still separated from God in the moment we are separated from our bodies, we will remain separated from God forever. As the heirs of Adam, separated from God, we all live life without God. That is the *law of sin and death* that works in our earthly human nature. Every problem you have during your stay on planet Earth will revolve around the *law of sin and death* that is working in your flesh. The *law of sin and death* is the human nature we are born with, inherited from Adam, with its tendency to sin (*live without God*). This spiritual tendency to live life without God is what causes physical death, which leads to eternal existence without God.

The Self Program

> And the serpent said unto the woman, Ye shall not surely die: For God doth know that in the day ye eat thereof, then your eyes shall be opened, and ye shall be as gods, knowing good and evil. (Genesis 3:4-5)

Our human problem of death began at the cradle of the human race in the Garden of Eden. It was there Satan preached to Eve his original *be your own god* philosophy, which is the root of religion. Satan told the human you can be your own god. In his political agenda he insinuated, "God doesn't love you; you don't need God. And rather than living for God and walking with God, you can live for the creature and have a whole world system that cares for the creature without God."

That at that time ye were without Christ, being aliens from the com-
monwealth of Israel, and strangers from the covenants of promise,
having no hope, and without God in the world. (Eph. 2:12)

As a result, we all live in a world without God and without hope. Satan
lied. He told us by getting knowledge we can be as gods. What Satan really
did was suggest to Eve to doubt God's love. He uprooted what was the
foundation of their relationship with God. They had seen God's power in
creation, they had tasted of the goodness of God and of fellowship with
God, but the love of God hadn't been fully revealed yet. That was the next
phase of spiritual growth they would have experienced as they ate of the
Tree of Life, but they never ate of the Tree of Life. Satan suggested God
didn't love them if He was withholding something from them but the only
thing God was withholding from them was death.

The truth is, a loving heavenly Father told them not to eat of that
tree because it would kill them. You would do the same for your kids. You
would say to them, "Look both ways before you cross the street, because
if you don't you will get run over by a car and it will kill you." A loving
God said to them, "Don't eat of that tree." The Tree of the Knowledge of
Good and Evil was in the midst of the Garden of Eden for a reason. It was
there to remind us that evil is present in the universe so don't be caught
off guard. God loved them by telling them to not eat of that tree just like
I would warn my son, saying, "Don't pick up that snake or you will get bit
and the poison will enter your bloodstream and cause you to die." Then
after they believed Satan's lie and disobeyed God, He came back into the
Garden seeking them as love would do. Wouldn't you search for your kids
even after they made a mess of things?

And I will put enmity between thee and the woman, and between
thy seed and her seed; it shall bruise thy head, and thou shalt
bruise his heel. (Genesis 3:15)

God immediately got involved. He promised Satan and them He would
reverse the curse through the seed of the woman. God said, "I will *put*." This
means the solution will be something God will do. It is going to come from
Heaven. He said, "I will put *enmity*." This means God will put someone on

earth who will deal violently with Satan. He said, "I will do it through the *seed* of the woman." This means a child of a virgin will be born that will come from Heaven. He will not be a child of Adam and have Adam's spiritual nature that is of the devil. He said to Satan, "You will bruise his heel, but he will crush your head." The only way to get rid of the danger of a snake is to cut off its head. This was the good news God preached to Adam and Eve and it is the foundation of all the promises of the Bible that men were believing God was going to do from that day forward. Then Adam and Eve watched God, in love, demonstrate how He would provide a remedy for their problem.

> Unto Adam also and to his wife did the LORD God make coats of skins, and clothed them. (Genesis 3:21)

God's first demonstration of His promised provision began with His act of killing innocent animals and covering Adam and Eve with their skins. God was showing them that just as He had killed innocent animals and clothed them with their coats of skins to cover their nakedness, even so one day He would send His innocent Son from Heaven. He would die in their place, and clothe them with His righteousness from God. They had sewed fig leaves together to make aprons to cover their nakedness but God was showing them nothing they could do would cover them of their spiritual nakedness. God had to cover them with the righteousness of another innocent being.

Satan's goal was to keep them from the knowledge of God and His love because that is what manifests eternal life. The knowledge of God's love is the only security for the guilty conscience. Knowledge without God is death. What Satan said to them about being your own gods was true if you are living life without God. The human certainly can use knowledge to be his own god. However, Satan lied by implying you can really live life without God. That is the satanic system, living life without God. That's like saying you have no need of God or His provisions. However, God is God, He always has been God and He always will be God. There is no world that God has created that can exist without God. There are only creatures that choose to live life with or without Him. God allows angels and humans to go their own way, but when you walk away from God you walk away from the eternal Tree of Life. God won't make us eat of His Tree of Life, but if we don't we will die. Adam walked away from God to be his own god. In so doing he basically sold our souls to the devil in order to have a temporary party without God.

> Furthermore, we have had fathers of our flesh, which corrected us, and we gave them reverence: shall we not much rather be in subjection unto the Father of spirits, and live? (Heb. 12:9)

Satan was the best politician in history. He came along with his agenda of a new world order of life without God and got Adam and Eve's vote. He became as the Bible says, the god of this world, and he has been running this world system ever since. History records the corruption of man and the destruction of empires that have risen and fallen without God. By getting Adam and Eve to participate in his agenda, he captured the human race within Adam's loins. Adam and Eve and all their children have been slaves of Satan ever since. How is that you ask? In Adam we all became programmed with Satan's self-program, which trains the human to be his own god. We live life without God and believe we can be our own gods without any repercussions. We believe in Satan's life without God world system. We think we are free to be *me* and the Bible says we are really in bondage to Satan. He is the great taskmaster who cracks his whip and says, "You will obey my lusts and serve my world system, without God." His deception is complete and the only one who can save us from *the great lie* is God. The world system is designed to build that deception into our hearts so we can be satisfied for a few short years, but our satisfaction is only temporary. God has designed our hearts to fellowship with Him and we will never be satisfied until we are safe living in God's presence again. If they would have obeyed God and had eaten of the Tree of Life, they would have gone to the next stage of eternal life, which is going from knowing God as God, to knowing God as Father.

> There is a way, which seemeth right unto a man, but the end thereof are the ways of death. (Prov. 14:12)

Satan lied when he said, "you shall not surely die." Satan was saying to them, "You can be free from God's boundaries of wisdom through the knowledge of good and evil." I'm sure you realize that knowing good and evil doesn't make us as gods, nor does it make us wise. Knowledge isn't evil. Knowledge without God is evil. That is part of the revelation of the two trees in the midst of the Garden of Eden. Believing Satan rather than God is evil. Living life without God is evil. A creation full of creatures out of control is evil. I guess you can see in today's world, no universe without God is safe. Without God in our life, we are doomed to remain a slave to Satan's self program all our lives. When the human loves life without rules, without standards, without boundaries, and without God, he is fully "free to be me" and in bondage to Satan's *be your own god* world system, but it always ends in destruction and death.

A Definition of S.E.L.F.

Satan's
Eternal
Love of
Folly

Self is the facemask of Satan for the human to wear in his lifestyle of sin. It's no wonder the devil says in every human "it's okay to be me" for the human in his lifestyle of sin. The Bible says living life without God and without any regard for eternity is folly.

> All we like sheep have gone astray; we have turned everyone to his own way. (Isa. 53:6a)

Sheep are the most helpless of animals when they go astray. God sees the human the same way. In Adam we believed Satan and joined his philosophy of living life without God. We've all turned to our own way, every one of us. This was the fall of man and it has been the way of man ever since. Each one of us pursues our own interests, makes our own plans and seeks to gratify our own selfishness without any regard to how it affects others.

Adam's choice to eat of the Tree of the Knowledge of Good and Evil was not only a choice to partake of Satan's program, but it was also a choice against God's program. When Adam walked away from God and submitted to Satan's agenda, he became born of Satan's spiritual nature and Satan became his spiritual father. Since every human being was in Adam, he became our spiritual father too. That is the way God sees us right now. It's like that in the natural. Dad has a kid and the kid grows up in Dad's image and carries on Dad's business. That is kind of what happened with Satan in the Garden of Eden.

> In whom the god of this world hath blinded the minds of them which believe not, lest the light of the glorious gospel of Christ, who is the image of God, should shine unto them. (2 Cor. 4:4)

The Bible says Satan is the god of this world. Satan's agenda is to be the god of this world, a position he wanted in Heaven when he was known as Lucifer. But Heaven is God's home and Jesus is the King of Heaven. As Lucifer, he once brought glory to God, but in his rebellion against God, his spiritual nature changed. When Lucifer rebelled against God and was kicked out of Heaven, his nature changed and he became known as Satan (which means opponent, adversary or enemy). As a fallen spirit separated from God, he saw God create the worlds and then give Adam the lordship over earth. Satan preached his agenda to Adam and Eve and they submitted to him. In obeying Satan, Adam's spiritual nature changed and we inherited his spiritual nature. Adam gave Satan his God-given lordship over the earth and over the human race, which became separated from God. Satan's world system without God through the self-program has ruled mankind ever since. The Bible teaches us there are two spiritual families, Satan and his kids vs. God with His kids. Each father has authority with their kids just like you have authority with your own kids. As in the natural so it is in the spiritual. God isn't going to come into a different family and take their kids. So what He did was send His Son to talk to us about God and His family, and then offer us the opportunity to come over into God's family and become God's kids. Isn't that great? That is part of the secret of eternity only found in the Bible. I know some of you might not like hearing about Satan, but he is your enemy and the Bible shows us Satan is our problem. He has been our problem since the Garden of Eden. Death is also our enemy. Death isn't part of God's program. Death originated with Satan. Life emanates from God.

For the love of money is the root of all evil: which while some coveted after, they have erred from the faith, and pierced themselves through with many sorrows. (1 Tim. 6:10)

To make matters worse, we are corrupt because we are programmed with Satan's self-program. We love living for self. It is the root of all evil. I know the scripture says *the love of money is the root of all evil*. But why is the love of money the root of all evil? It is so we can be our own gods and live for self. The money system is what empowers us in this life to make provision for our own godhood.

No one can serve two masters; for either he will hate the one and love the other, or else he will be loyal to the one and despise the other. You cannot serve God and mammon (the money system). (Matt. 6:24)

There is nothing wrong with money. Money could be used to meet everyone's need and everyone would be cared for. It is the love of money so we can be all that we can be without God that is the root of all evil. If we include God in our lives money is perfectly fine. As natural humans we live to be our own gods and do whatever we want. The Bible says *all seek their own*. Every man lives for himself. That is the root of all evil. On a worldly level humans band together to have a world system without God and run the world however they want. But the inspiration behind it all is Satan. You can see this fact when Satan approached Jesus in the wilderness.

And the devil said unto him, if thou be the Son of God, command this stone that it be made bread. And Jesus answered him, saying, *it is written, that man shall not live by bread alone, but by every word of God.* And the devil, taking him up into an high mountain, shewed unto him all the kingdoms of the world in a moment of time. And the devil said unto him, all this power will I give thee, and the glory of them: for that is delivered unto me; and to whomsoever I will I give it. If thou therefore wilt worship me, all shall be thine. And Jesus answered and said unto him, *get thee behind me, Satan: for it is*

written, Thou shalt worship the Lord thy God, and him only shalt thou serve.
(Luke 4:3-8)

In a moment of time Satan showed Jesus all the kingdoms of this world and then he said, "This power was given unto me and I can give it to whomever I want." Jesus didn't argue with Satan about the fact that Adam had given the lordship over planet Earth to him. Jesus basically told Satan, "God is God *and you are not* and I don't need what your system provides."

Forasmuch then as the children are partakers of flesh and blood, he also himself likewise took part of the same; that through death he might destroy him that had the power of death, that is, the devil. (Heb. 2:14)

Jesus wasn't born of Adam's sin nature and He didn't activate Satan's self program in His heart. He was born of a virgin by the power of the Spirit of God so He didn't have Adam's blood with the sin nature in Him. *Jesus came from Heaven to Earth to reverse the curse for us.* The creation is out of submission to God and God sent Jesus to set spiritual laws in motion to bring all things back into God's order. Look what Jesus told Pontius Pilate.

Jesus answered, *My kingdom is not of this world: if my kingdom were of this world, then would my servants fight, that I should not be delivered to the Jews: but now is my kingdom not from hence.* Pilate therefore said unto him, Art thou a king then? Jesus answered; *Thou sayest that I am a king. To this end was I born, and for this cause came I into the world, that I should bear witness unto the truth. Every one that is of the truth heareth my voice.* Pilate saith unto him, What is truth? And when he had said this, he went out again unto the Jews, and saith unto them, I find in him no fault at all. (John 18:36-38)

What is truth? I think, in this world, that is the greatest question ever asked. Pontius Pilate asked Jesus that question right before he declared Jesus to be without fault and then handed Him over to the Jews to be crucified. This question is one of my eight favorite unanswered questions I have found in the Bible, which leads men back to God. What is truth for you?

Jesus came from Heaven to earth to tell us the truth. Jesus constantly taught that He came from Heaven to earth, that His heavenly Father sent Him, that He came to show us the life and to tell us the truth.

> For all seek their own, not the things which are Jesus Christ's.
> (Phil. 2:21)

The kingdoms of this world are founded upon the lie that men can be their own gods and have a world without God. That is Satan's agenda and political structure. Every new world order testifies of a world without God filled with men who are programmed by the corrupt self program. And history records the evil of creation without God. Man cannot change his spiritual nature. He lives for self and nobody else. Jesus doesn't live for self, but for the heavenly Father and all His creation. Jesus came to show us the difference between the Self program (which is death) and the Son program (which is life). God can't take us out of the self program. However, God can cause us to be born again of the SON program. The only way to get Satan's death program of self out of us is by God downloading the SON program into us. We can't do that. Only God can do that. He created us and only He can re-create us. That is what God offers to do for us in the Bible.

> Behold therefore the goodness and severity of God: on them which fell, severity; but toward thee, goodness, if thou continue in His goodness: otherwise thou also shalt be cut off. And they also, if they abide not still in unbelief, shall be grafted in: for God is able to graft them in again. For if thou wert cut out of the olive tree which is wild by nature, and wert grafted contrary to nature into a good olive tree: how much more shall these, which be the natural branches, be grafted into their own olive tree?
> (Rom. 11:22-24)

The Bible uses the example of how one can change the nature of a tree by grafting the tree with a piece of another tree. That is exactly what God does with us through Jesus. God will graft the divine nature of His Son Jesus into us if we will ask Him to, through the cursed tree of the cross. The New Testament explains how Jesus died for us and was punished in our place for the sins we commit through the self program. The Bible teaches us how Jesus removed sin from us on the cross, and how He removes the self program from us, as we abide in the Son program. It isn't just the sins that make us unfit for Heaven, but it is also the self that commits the sins (the Bible calls it sin).

What Is Sin?

The word *sin* sounds like a strange word because we don't use it much in our generation. The Bible talks about it a lot. The Hebrew word for sin is *chattâ'âh* and it means *"missing the road or missing the mark."* It is erring from the way of God. The Bible teaches the way of God is love, so when you are out of love, you are sinning. Sin is going your own way and not in God's way. Sin is the wall that stands between you and God. Sin is the tendency to live life without God. It is our tendency to be our own god, and to think I have no need for God or His purpose. God is offended with that philosophy and that agenda because sin violates the royal law (the mark) of God's kingdom, which is love. He is God and we are not. His law of love is the surety and security of God's kingdom. Anything in His universe that isn't willing to flow in God's divine order of love, which He has designed and ordained, is offensive to God and will not be allowed in Heaven. Everybody sins against God but God has made provision for us through Jesus Christ so we can be cleansed of sin.

It's like weeds overgrowing your house. If you don't destroy the weeds they will destroy your house. The same is true about sin. God doesn't allow sin in His universe or in Heaven. It's pretty wise of God to open up a window of time in eternity as a trial period in a practice realm known as earth to develop His family for Heaven. When the rule of law is love, then any attitude that is against love towards God or others is sin. In the Bible, those who don't know God and live only for self are called sinners. Sin is the spiritual problem and it is the source of all the problems in the natural universe. The Bible talks about sin (the inward sin nature) and sins (the outward actions of the sin nature) a lot.

He that committeth sin is of the devil; for the devil sinneth from the beginning. For this purpose the Son of God was manifested, that he might *destroy the works of the devil.* (1 John 3:8)

Sin has eternal consequences and God gave the Law to hold us responsible for our sins, but by the grace of God He also provided a way of escape from the consequences of sin. The animal sacrifices in the Old Testament are God's way of teaching us about sin and how He has provided a remedy for sin through His Son, Jesus. God loved us before we were born and He sent Jesus from Heaven to earth to deal with the sin problem so we can all have a relationship with God. I like to simplify it by saying it like this:

Sin is the human:

- ✔ Being his own god
- ✔ Doing his own will
- ✔ Going his own way
- ✔ Living for self

A Description of the Nature of S.I.N.

Satan
In
Nature

Sin originated with the devil. Sin is Satan's spiritual nature. To make it simple I say it is Satan's operating system. The Bible tells us Satan's nature entered into the world by one man. We were all in Adam when Adam sinned, and when he sinned, we all became sinners. We have all inherited the spiritual nature of our father Adam. We are all born with Adam's self nature. It was the same operating system Satan tried to install in Heaven among the angels when he was known as Lucifer. Sin was revealed in Lucifer among all the angels in Heaven and he was removed from Heaven along with all the other angels that chose Lucifer's path. When Lucifer's spiritual nature changed, his name became Satan who then introduced sin into planet Earth and separated the human race from God.

> Wherefore, as by one man sin entered into the world, and death by sin; and so death passed upon all men, for that all have sinned. (Rom. 5:12)

Sin separates the human from God because sin is the lifestyle of living without God or living outside of God's authority. That's what makes Satan who he is. God will not allow sin in His presence in Heaven. God loves us, but He hates sin. God will destroy sin and its effects throughout the whole universe, but He has made a way possible for us to be saved. That's the good news of the Bible. Sin puts us in a tough position because every soul born of Adam is filled with the rebel sin nature disguised as self. The Bible says sin entered the race *by one man* and death by sin, so *death passed upon all men* for all men have sinned. This makes us incompatible with God, unfit for Heaven and headed for the fire that burns every evil thing up forever.

Separated from God

> Then when lust hath conceived, it bringeth forth sin: and sin, when it is finished, bringeth forth death. (Jas. 1:15)

As Adam's descendants, his fallen nature is in us all, except one. Jesus was born of a virgin and had a different Father so His spiritual nature was God's divine nature. When Adam died spiritually, we all died spiritually and now because we are born spiritually dead, we die physically. If we are spiritually dead when we die physically we shall remain dead (separated from God) forever. The only one that has the power to save us from death is God. He has done that through Jesus Christ. God doesn't want any of us to die. God loves us and wants us to live. That's why He sent Jesus from Heaven to earth to show us the solution. Jesus has conquered death for us. You don't have to die. That is why God wrote the Bible, to show us His heavenly solution to our earthly problem through

His only Son Jesus Christ. God is a good God and He created all things for His purpose. Death was not a part of God's original plan. Death is an enemy of man and an enemy of God. This is the dominant theme of the Bible.

The Natural Man

> Howbeit that was not first which is spiritual, but that which is natural; and afterward that which is spiritual. (1 Cor. 15:46)

This is another one of the eight questions I have found in the Bible that lead men to eternal life. The Bible calls the human, born of Adam, that is separated from God, the natural man. In all the Scriptures, the human race is divided into two groups: the natural man and the spiritual man. The question goes, "Howbeit?" Like Nicodemus said, "How can these things be?" Adam walked away from God and when he did he became a natural man. His spirit died. As a natural man he has not the life of God in him. As a result, all his offspring are natural men. Man was supposed to eat of the Tree of Life and be made alive spiritually but he disobeyed God and died. So that which is first is not spiritual but natural. But then the scripture goes on to say, afterwards comes the spiritual man. If we will respond to God in our hearts, we can become spiritual. Just like a seed is a natural dead thing, but out of it springs a living tree, even so our bodies are dead seeds from which a spiritual man can be born. God has provided us with His Son who is the spiritual man. When we believe in Jesus, who is *the last Adam*, His Spirit quickens us and out of our dead cold hearts springs a new living tree.

> But the natural man receiveth not the things of the Spirit of God: for they are foolishness unto him: neither can he know them, because they are spiritually discerned. (1 Cor. 2:1)

A natural man cannot beget a spiritual man. We cannot make ourselves spiritual. God is God and not we ourselves. God created us and only God can re-create us. God does this through the last Adam, which is Jesus Christ. Just like Adam was the natural seed of the human race and he became a tree of sinners, even so God has provided us with the last Adam, Christ who is the spiritual seed that becomes for us the Tree of Life. We can connect with Jesus and become born again of a new program that imparts His divine nature to us. It doesn't make us perfect while we are on earth, but it puts us in the spiritual man and changes our spiritual character so when we physically die, the self program will drop off and the only thing that will remain is Christ in us.

> For if ye live after the flesh, ye shall die: but if ye through the Spirit do mortify the deeds of the body, ye shall live. (Rom. 8:13)

The Bible says if we live by the natural man for self, we will die. When we love *the n*atural man so much that we think the things of the Spirit of God are foolishness, then we fail to grasp the knowledge of God and we choose to not activate our rights to the life of *the spiritual man*. If we come to Jesus within our hearts and have faith in what God says He has done for us in the Bible, Jesus brings us back into right relationship with God. Through Christ in us we are made alive unto God by His Spirit and are born again of His divine nature. By the Spirit of Christ in us, our deeds (our ways) begin to be mortified (put to death) so we can truly live and walk in God's presence.

We Can't Save Ourselves

> That at that time ye were without Christ, being aliens from the commonwealth of Israel, and strangers from the covenants of promise, having no hope, and without God in the world. (Eph. 2:12)

As mere humans, we naturally tend to think we can just do good things and God will appreciate that and save us, but according to the Bible, that is the furthest thing from the truth. The Bible says we are lost, without hope, and without God in this world and we can't save ourselves (see Eph. 2:12). God is the only one who can save us. God doesn't want anyone to die and be lost. He never did. The only solution to our human problem of death is life (union with God). He alone can save us.

Religion teaches another way. Religion teaches man can earn his salvation through some sort of good works system that will make up for his evil deeds and for the rest of his life he must hope his religion works. Even Christianity doesn't work as a religion because man's focus is upon his own goodness rather than the goodness of God. Man cannot buy what Jesus has already paid for like Cain tried to do through good works and was rejected. Doing good works to earn God's respect is a way other than God's way.

> The heart is deceitful above all things, and desperately wicked: who can know it? (Jer. 17:9)

Doing good deeds, being a good person, giving money to the church or charities, water baptism, and many other things men trust in to save them, cannot earn Heaven. We don't deserve Heaven and we can't earn Heaven. We deceive ourselves constantly. Living life without God is the fountain of deception. You probably wouldn't take out a loan on a product you knew was defective. You probably wouldn't have kids without thinking you will have some sort of benefit by having children. So why would you be faithful to some religion that brainwashes you to do things with your heart that doesn't produce what you want, which is Heaven? Men all over the world will believe all kinds of lies and do all kinds of deeds to satisfy their religion but God wants a personal relationship with the creature He created and He has made that possible for us. When it comes to eternity, religion demands we invest our most important asset, our soul's eternal destiny, on a hope, a prayer, and some good works. Man cannot provide the remedy to his problem because he is the one who is in bondage to the problem. Man cannot overcome Satan because he is under Satan's dominion. Man cannot change his spiritual nature because he is without the power to create a new spiritual nature. The Son of God came and conquered Satan for us. When we come to Him and trust in Him, His victory over Satan, sin and death becomes ours.

> Can the Ethiopian change his skin, or the leopard his spots? Then may ye also do good, that are accustomed to do evil. (Jer. 13:23)

The Bible says it would be easier for an Ethiopian to change the color of his skin, or for a leopard to get rid of his spots, than for a natural man to change his sinful nature. The reason is because his heart is desperately wicked and as one scripture says full of deadly poison. So religion provides man with the infidel of reason instead of the supernatural power of God. The reasoning of religion cannot possibly change the human heart enough to bring him back into fellowship with God, but God can change our hearts.

> Forasmuch then as the children are partakers of flesh and blood, he also himself likewise took part of the same; that through death he might *destroy him that had the power of death*, that is, the devil. (Heb. 2:14)

The Bible is totally opposite of religion. The Bible teaches we don't deserve salvation, nor can we earn salvation and we don't have the supernatural power in ourselves to overcome death. The Bible teaches only God, Himself, can deliver us from death and that we must trust in the goodness of God that He has done that for us through His only Son who took upon Himself our death problem so we could live. God, in His goodness, promised Adam and Eve a solution. The Bible is that historical document which shows us how God has historically provided His solution, that delivers us from Satan's power of death. The more you study the Bible and the better you understand the human problem from God's perspective, the more you will marvel at God's solution.

Personal Study Notes

GOD HAS PROVIDED *the* SOLUTION

But when the fullness of the time was come,
God sent forth his Son, made of a woman, made under the law,
To redeem them that were under the law, that we might
receive the adoption of sons.

G A L . 4 : 4 - 5

The Paradise of Eden

Now remember this. God doesn't just do things. God does everything for a purpose. God does nothing without accomplishing His purpose. In everything God does, He teaches something. God never does anything without teaching something. God says it, then God does it, and then God reveals it.

Remember, the message of the Bible is the same gospel that was preached in the Old Testament as was preached in the New Testament. It is the revelation of God's purpose for creation. It is the good news of the heavenly provision that a loving God has made through His only Son, to recover man out of the state of death into which he had fallen and to bring him back into the glorious state of life and fellowship, fulfilling His purpose of creation.

> But now is Christ risen from the dead, and become the firstfruits of them that slept. For since by man came death, by man came also the resurrection of the dead. For as in Adam all die, even so in Christ shall all be made alive. (1 Cor. 15:20-22)

Walking with God in the Garden of Eden was Paradise, a picture of the way life is supposed to be. There was innocence. There was peace. There was glory. God and man were friends. That is the life that God promised us and that's what eternal life is. Man had responsibilities given to him by God to take care of the planet and subdue all enemies. God made regular visits to fellowship with man. The earth was a paradise without the curse, without disease, without bad weather, without thorns and briars, without dangerous animals, without corrupt hearts, death and destruction. Everything in the plant kingdom, the animal kingdom, and the human kingdom was good and was filled with the glory of God.

We see that man was quite intelligent, being able to name all the animals, as God instructed him. God joined the man and woman together so that they were one flesh, one in heart, one in mind, one in purpose, one in destiny. Life with God is supposed to be a paradise just like life in Heaven is paradise, as we become one with God. The life was promised and provided for us as long as the human race followed God's instructions and stayed within God's boundaries for the good of all creation fulfilling God's royal law of love. God did His part and the race was in position with God to do its part.

Paradise Was Lost

> And so it is written, the first man Adam was made a living soul; the last Adam was made a quickening spirit. Howbeit that was not first which is spiritual, but that which is natural; and afterward that which is spiritual. The first man is of the earth, earthy: the second man is the Lord from heaven. (1 Cor. 15:45-47)

All was lost when the fellowship was broken. History has been recording the consequences of what a world is like when fellowship with the Creator is broken and the creation is in full sin-mode.

The first man is of the earth, and his spiritual nature is earthy. As the offspring of Adam we all partake of his spiritual nature. Because he never ate of the Tree of Life he failed to enter into the program of immortality God had planned for him and man is now limited to being a mere mortal, a creature of earth. All Adam had to do was walk with God, follow God's instructions, and eat of the Tree of Life. God was giving Adam the opportunity to put on immortality by eating of the Tree of Life. Had Adam done that, the Spirit of God would have quickened him with eternal life and paradise would have continued. Adam made the wrong choice and that choice affected all his unborn children, which includes you and me. In the above passage of scripture, the Bible calls him the first Adam. This implies there is another Adam. The Bible calls Christ the last Adam. This means there is no other. The word Adam means species. The first Adam implies the first one in whom the race partakes. The last Adam implies the last one in whom the race can partake.

The first Adam separated the race from God. In like manner the last Adam, Jesus Christ, brings us back to God. Just as we partook of the inheritance provided by Adam, even so we can partake of the inheritance provided by Christ Jesus. As the offspring of Adam we inherit his relationship with God, which is death (judgment, condemnation and eternal separation from

God). As children of God in Christ we inherit His relationship with God, which is life (righteousness, fellowship with God and partakers of His divine nature). We can make the right choice. The message of the Bible is, we can go from death to life, from Adam to Christ and from Satan to God by faith.

> Therefore if any man be in Christ, he is a new creature: old things are passed away; behold, all things are become new. (2 Cor. 5:17)

Jesus was born of Mary, but not of the blood line of Adam. Jesus was the Son of Man (with a human body), but He was also the Son of God (with God's Spirit). You may think it strange for God to bring forth a man from a woman's body only, but in the Garden of Eden, God brought forth a woman from a man's body only. Jesus was the God man. Just as we partake of Adam's spiritual nature, we can partake of Jesus' spiritual nature. This is part of the overall theme of the Bible. Adam embraced a philosophy of life that originated with Satan, which causes separation from God and in doing so he took in Satan's spiritual nature of enmity against God. The whole world system is built on that spiritual philosophy of living life without God. The same principle in reverse is true of Jesus who is the last Adam. Jesus' philosophy of life is that of son-ship with God. Jesus did nothing for self.

Jesus only did what he saw His Father do. Jesus constantly preached that. He said "My words are not mine, but they are from the heavenly Father who sent me." He said, "The Father in me doeth the works, the Son can do nothing of self, but only what He sees the Father do." He said, "He that believeth in me has already passed from death to life." Jesus always talked about death and life. God sent Jesus to be the last Adam. Jesus is the head of a new race with the divine nature. We are one species of being in Adam but we are a new species of being in Christ. God is able to put us in Christ just like He put us in Adam. God created us, and God alone can recreate us. Jesus was crucified because He claimed to be the Son of God. But the Bible says in the book of Isaiah, chapter 55, Jesus was stricken, smitten of God and afflicted so we could become the children of God.

God Made Us the Promise

> And I will put enmity between thee and the woman, and between thy seed and her seed; it shall bruise thy head, and thou shalt bruise his heel. (Genesis 3:15)

The first thing God did when man fell was to make us a promise. This first promise from God is the cornerstone upon which all the promises of God are founded. Here God says, I will send a savior by the power of God, who will overcome Satan and deliver you from his powers of death. When He comes Satan will bruise His heel but He is going to crush Satan's head and remove Satan's dominion of sin and death over man. He will come through the seed of the woman by virgin birth. That is impossible! Nothing is impossible for God. That is the heart of the lesson of the Bible. Only God can save us and He promised to save us through His only Son. Jesus came from Heaven to earth as a spiritual surgeon to remove all offenses from us so we could come back to God.

Throughout the Bible God gives us clues in blood, pointing us to the manifestation of His only Son. God begins in this passage of scripture by promising them (and us in them) a savior. This is the original blood covenant called the Adamic Covenant. God's first promise to us was that He would deal with the one that has the power of death, which is the devil. He told Satan in front of Adam and Eve He was going to put His Son into earth by virgin birth (seed of the woman) and that Satan would cause Him pain but the Son would destroy Satan's dominion over man forever. I like the translation from the Amplified Bible, which quotes,

> And I will put enmity between you and the woman, and between your offspring and her offspring; He will bruise and tread your head underfoot, and you will lie in wait and bruise His heel. (Genesis 3:15, AMP)

God was telling them and us that the headship of the first creation would come back to God by hostile takeover, through His only Son who would be her offspring. This is not only the first promise that became the cornerstone of all the promises of God, but it was also the first prophecy that built faith in their hearts for their future deliverance. Satan took dominion (headship) over the creation by hostile takeover the way a serpent swallows its prey whole. But the Son of God would become the son of man to bring the creation back to God by hostile takeover. The original Hebrew word for the word "enmity" is the word *eba*, pronounced a-bah, and it means "hostility, hatred." The Bible is saying this will be the attitude between Jesus and Satan concerning the dominion over the creation. It's also the hatred and hostility between God's people and Satan's people. We see this enmity between the righteous and the wicked, beginning with Cain and Abel, all the way through the Bible. This first original promise from God fixed the hope of their hearts towards the one that would be born of the virgin and reverse the curse. All future promises from God are founded upon this first promise.

Adam chose to go with Satan's agenda rather than obey God's instructions. Adam fell from his exalted position of fellowship with God and lord of creation and every soul fell with Adam. That includes you and me. In bowing the knee to Satan's program, Adam gave his God-given dominion over creation to the devil and Satan became, as the Bible says, the god of this world. Jesus called Satan the prince of this world. The apostle Paul called Satan the prince of the power of the air, the spirit that now works in the children of disobedience. God knew this would happen but planned before creation to provide us with the way back home through His only Son.

God saw Satan pull that stunt among the angels in Heaven in ages past when he was known then as Lucifer. God knew Satan would challenge Adam also. After the fall of Adam and Eve, which brought the curse upon the universe, God began His plan with Adam and Eve by promising He would send a Savior from Heaven. He would be born as the seed of the woman (virgin womb), conquer Satan (empty tomb), and destroy Satan's dominion of death over man. Jesus was the miracle child that was born of the virgin. Jesus was God's Son that He promised to give for us. Jesus is the Savior of the world. He has conquered death for us. He is the one that has destroyed Satan's death-power over us and has opened the door of Heaven to us. Jesus brings us back to God so we can have eternal life, which Adam lost for us. Jesus came from Heaven to Earth to tell us about the life, to show us the life, and to make possible our entry into the life that is lived in Heaven.

That day in the garden, God said to Satan, "I will put." This means only God can do it and it will come from Heaven. He said "I will put enmity." The Greek definition of this word means *hostility*. It means Satan will have his hands full because the one that is coming from God will violently deal with Satan by hostile force. He said, "I will put enmity between you and her and between your seed and her seed." That means Jesus is going to come through a virgin and be the offspring of God. It also means there will be enmity between the children of Adam and the children of God. This hostility is seen clearly throughout the Bible beginning with Cain and Abel and it continues today between the godly and the ungodly. People who are hostile towards Christians may not know why. They just don't like them but it is the enmity that the Bible talks about. Examine your heart and see if you dislike Christians. The enmity of your own heart will guarantee your separation from God.

Finally, He said to Satan, "you will bruise his heel but he will crush your head." That means the Savior is going suffer but He is going to take the keys of death, Hell, and the grave away from Satan. It means He will take Satan's authority over all creation away and destroy his powers of death over mankind. Now that is the good news of the Bible, which can be found in no religion on earth. That is the power of God promised to us.

God Gave Us the Sign

> Therefore, the Lord himself shall give you a sign; Behold, *a virgin shall conceive*, and bear a son, and shall call his name Immanuel. (Isa. 7:14)

The promise God gave Adam and Eve was *the seed of the woman*. The sign God gave the human race is the son of the *virgin womb* that gave us the *empty tomb*. The sign God gave the prophet Isaiah to show us was the same sign He gave Abraham and Sarah in old age and a barren womb. They had a miracle child that was promised to them by the power of God. The supernatural demonstrations of God's power in the Old Testament pointed us to the miracle child He promised would be born of a virgin for the purpose of crushing the head of the serpent, in order to loose man from Satan's dominion.

> Now the birth of Jesus Christ was as follows: After His mother Mary was betrothed to Joseph, before they came together, she was found with child of the Holy Spirit. Then Joseph her husband, being a just man, and not wanting to make her a public example, was minded to put her away secretly. But while he thought about these things, behold, an angel of the Lord appeared to him in a dream, saying, "Joseph, son of David, do not be afraid to take to you Mary your wife, for that which is conceived in her is of the Holy Spirit. And she will bring forth a Son, and you shall call His name JESUS, for He will save His people from their sins." So all this was done that it might be fulfilled which was spoken by the Lord through the prophet, saying: "Behold, the virgin shall be with child, and bear a Son, and they shall call His name Immanuel," which is translated, "*God with us.*" (Matt. 1:18-23 NKJV)

The virgin birth was impossible for man but that is part of the lesson of the Bible. Only God can do the impossible. This is where mere religion falls short. The God of the Bible promised to do the impossible for mankind. If the Spirit of God can create a universe like we see Him do in the first two chapters of the Bible, is anything too hard for God? He can create a body for His Son Jesus in the womb of a virgin and He can create a new heart in you. All the miracle children in the Old Testament were pictures and signs of the miracle child that would come to fulfill God's first promise of Genesis 3:15.

God has demonstrated His powers throughout history and He is a historical God. Why wouldn't He be? God created time! But the miracle child is the greatest sign God has ever given us. Man could not have a child with the divine nature. Only God could have a child with His divine nature. God did this in a virgin called Mary. In this way the child didn't have the spiritual nature of Adam. God was His Father. Well that isn't as hard to believe as we think. Do we find it hard to believe we were born? No! Well the same God who created the human created a body for His Son in the womb of a virgin and His name is Jesus.

> Wherefore when he cometh into the world, he saith, Sacrifice and offering thou wouldest not, but *a body hast thou prepared me:* In burnt offerings and sacrifices for sin thou hast had no pleasure. Then said I, Lo, I come (*in the volume of the book it is written of me,*) to do thy will, O God. (Heb. 10:5-7)

The Son was talking to His Father God before He was born, saying, "I come for you, Father." God provided a body for Jesus and Jesus provided His obedience so God could do supernatural surgery upon the broken human race in Christ. He came for me and for you. Everything Jesus said and did, He did to please the Father and He did it for our sake.

God Sent Us the Son

> For God *so loved* the world, that *he gave* his only begotten Son, that *whosoever believeth* in him should not perish, but have everlasting life. (John 3:16)

Notice this passage of scripture says, "God so loved." Wow. Then it says "God gave His Only Son so we might not perish." Wow. It says if we believe in His Son we *should not* perish. Wow. No religion or belief system on the earth, designed by man or angel, can compete with the love of God found only in the Bible. All the religions of the world teach man must do it all, while the Bible teaches God did it all. Religion teaches man must do something for God, but the Bible teaches God must do something for broken man. Religion teaches, man must become a better human, but the Bible teaches, man must become a new creature. Religion teaches, man has the power to make himself a better person, but the Bible teaches it is impossible for man to become a better person. Religion teaches, man must do good works to make up for his evil deeds, but the Bible teaches, man needs a Savior and God has supernaturally provided one for us in His Son Jesus

Christ, as His free gift of love to all mankind. Religions teach concepts of men and so-called angels, but the Bible teaches the love of God, the goodness of God, the provision of God and the power of God for every creature. Religions promise life but end in death. The Bible teaches God gave His only Son to die for us that whosoever believes in Him should not perish but have eternal life. Religion teaches things that cannot be proven, but the Bible has proven its teachings by the historical resurrection of Jesus Christ. The Bible has never been disproven or exhausted. The Bible is the only source of miracles, signs, wonders, and resurrections. God wrote the Bible for us. God sent His Son for us. Isn't that amazing?

> For unto us *a child is born*, unto us *a son is given*: and the government shall be upon his shoulder: and his name shall be called Wonderful, Counselor, the Mighty God, the Everlasting Father, the Prince of Peace. (Isa. 9:6)

In this passage of scripture, God's gift to us was a twofold deal.

A Child Was Born. He could represent man because He has a flesh body. That's why He has the title of Son of Man, because He is in the family of man.

A Son Was Given. He could represent God because He has God's Spirit. That's why He has the title of Son of God, because He has always existed with the heavenly Father. This puts Him in position to establish God's government on earth. He left Heaven, came to earth and opened up the way for us, so when we leave earth, we can go to Heaven.

> Forasmuch then as the children are partakers of flesh and blood, he also himself likewise took part of the same; that through death he might destroy him that had the power of death, that is, the devil; And deliver them who through fear of death were all their lifetime subject to bondage. (Heb. 2:14-15)

It was a messy job, but somebody with the power of God had to do it. God has sent Jesus from Heaven to work things out for us. He has come and has shown us what eternal life looks like. He fulfilled God's plan and He has opened the doors of Heaven to us. God is having His family just as He originally purposed and God's plan of creation is working perfectly just as He planned. Through Jesus, God is creating a new species of being which never existed before. Out of all tribes and tongues, peoples, and cultures God is developing a new race, which lives by His divine nature, compatible with God and fit for Heaven.

For God to provide His solution to man's death problem, Jesus had to come from Heaven to infuse the race with the power of God. The Bible says through Jesus Christ death has been swallowed up in Life. He became *the son of man* so we could become *the sons of God*. He overcame death for us that we might partake of His life. Hopefully the following three principles will help you understand the solution that God presents to us through *the operation of God* in the Bible.

- ✔ Something must die that I might live
- ✔ God covers all by that which has died
- ✔ I only live by that which is raised

Death, Life and Resurrection covers the needs of the human from God's perspective. These three principles present the theme of the Bible, which is God's provision for every soul to have eternal life through Jesus Christ, the Lamb of God. As we progress in the Old Testament, you will be able to see the theme of the Bible God is trying to paint into our minds so we can receive from God the measure of faith and believe the truth.

1. Something Must Die That I Might Live

> And the eyes of them both were opened, and they knew that they were naked; and they sewed fig leaves together, and made themselves aprons. (Genesis 3:7)

After Adam and Eve sinned against God they discerned they were naked of the glory they used to walk in before God. Their focus was no longer upon God in the spiritual but upon themselves in the natural. What they were feeling was their spiritual death of separation from God. They felt the need to cover themselves, so they began to do good works to make up for their sin by sewing fig leaves together to make aprons that would cover their nakedness. Man's ability to feel his separation from God is what motivates him to do good works to please God. This shows man's natural tendency to make up for the bad by doing something good. They began to depend upon themselves rather than God. But man's need requires a supernatural solution that man cannot accomplish. Relationship with God is for the purpose of fellowship with God. We were created for eternity.

> Neither is there any creature that is not manifest in his sight: but all things are naked and opened unto the eyes of him with whom we have to do. (Heb. 4:13)

When God returned to the Garden, they were afraid and ashamed and they blamed each other, but they had worked together to clothe themselves of their nakedness, which they felt before God. He basically told them, "No, you cannot cover yourself through good works. You can't earn my favor and you don't deserve my presence, but I will cover you." This is the heart of the message of the Bible wrapped up in God's first promise to us in Genesis 3:15. We cannot clothe ourselves in the kind of righteousness that merits fellowship with God. Without the power of God, we are incompatible with God, unfit for Heaven and headed for Hell.

> Unto Adam also and to his wife did the LORD God make coats of skins, and clothed them. (Genesis 3:21)

Before creation, God planned our provision of eternal life. This life was to be offered to us through God's only Son. God *demonstrated* to them His promise in Genesis 3:15 by killing innocent animals and covering Adam and Eve with their skins. God was teaching them something must die that they might live. One of the greatest clues God shows us throughout the Bible of His promise to give us eternal life is the perfect, innocent, sacrificial lamb.

> For by grace are ye saved through faith; and that not of yourselves: it is the gift of God: Not of works, lest any man should boast. (Eph. 2:8-9)

God was promising them to send His Son to be our innocent sacrificial Lamb of God. In this way God was teaching Adam and Eve that just as the innocent animals died in their place to take their punishment for sin and their skins were provided to cover them of their nakedness and shame before God, even so His righteous Son would one day come and be our innocent sacrificial lamb. He would die in our place, take our punishment for sin, cover our nakedness before God and clothe us with His own righteousness. God was saying, "You don't deserve this right standing with God and you can't earn God's love, which the Son has always enjoyed, but by grace (the goodness of God), through faith (believing His operation), you will be saved (restored to fellowship and righteous standing with God again)."

When God killed those animals in front of them, He was demonstrating to them how the promise would be fulfilled. This practice of approaching God with an innocent sacrificial lamb has been practiced by all believers in the Old Testament ever since. Through this practice, men demonstrated their belief in God's promise that an innocent being would be provided that would become their substitute in death so they can walk before God again in the innocence of the one who died for them. Men have borrowed this practice to offer all kinds of sacrifices to the gods of their religions throughout the ages, but the Bible is where it all began. Religion makes untrue promises that you can work your way into favor with God but the Bible continues its theme of God's promise that *He will provide a Savior for us* without our help.

> Saying with a loud voice, Worthy is the Lamb that was slain to receive power, and riches, and wisdom, and strength, and honour, and glory, and blessing. (Rev. 5:12)

From the beginning Jesus is called the Lamb of God. In all the Gospels when you read and see the focus of Jesus, you will see that His only purpose was to show us eternal life and to give us eternal life. Everything Jesus taught centered on His destiny of dying on the cross so we could come to Heaven. To Jesus it was as good as done. Jesus' first sermon was summed up in the words of Matthew 3:2 where He said, "Repent ye: for the kingdom of heaven is at hand." When Jesus entered the ministry saying that, He was saying, "Get ready to change the way you think and the way you live because Heaven has invaded earth, and through the power of God I'm going to the cross for you so you can come to the Kingdom of Heaven with me." Notice Heaven is not a democracy. Heaven is a Kingdom and Heaven has a King. Jesus talked as if everything He was going to do for us was already done. Before creation, God called those things which are not as though they were. God called Jesus the Lamb of God slain before the foundation of the world for us that we might live. God knew before creation what would happen in Eden and how it would affect all of Adam's unborn children and God met our every need through the Lamb of God.

2. God Covers All By That Which Has Died

> The next day John seeth Jesus coming unto him, and saith, Behold the Lamb of God, which taketh away the sin of the world . . . And looking upon Jesus as he walked, he saith, Behold the Lamb of God! (John 1:29,36)

When God killed the innocent animals, He was showing Adam and Eve an innocent creature must die in their place. Then when God covered Adam and Eve with their skins He was showing them that they would be covered with the righteousness of the innocent substitute. This is exactly how God so loved the world that He gave His only Son that whosoever believes might not perish but have eternal life. Jesus was as innocent as a lamb. He is called in the Bible the Lamb of God. The innocent sacrificial lamb is God's picture to us of Jesus as our substitute. He took our punishment that we might be given His righteous standing with God.

> By faith Abel offered unto God a more excellent sacrifice than Cain, by which he obtained witness that he was righteous, God testifying of his gifts: and by it he being dead yet speaketh. (Heb. 11:4)

Then we see the innocent lamb again with Abel. He was taught by his parents to come to God by the shed blood of an innocent sacrificial lamb thereby pleasing God. This natural law signifies the spiritual law that *something must die so we might live.* In the Old Testament, the greatest mental picture of the Savior was the perfect innocent sacrificial lamb. God chose the lamb to be the animal, to best represent His perfect innocent Son, Jesus Christ. The pattern of the lamb is that the innocent lamb must die so we might live. The Bible says in the book of Revelation Jesus was the Lamb slain before the foundation of the world. The Bible teaches that the heavenly Father and His Son planned before creation that Jesus would come to earth to secure God's family after the man freely chose separation from God. God wrote the Bible over time, and used actual events in the Old Testament to be patterns, figures, types and examples, as mental pictures that would later become revelations to us in the New Testament. In the Old Testament, God used historical events, places, people and things, to point to His provision in the future. Now through the New Testament teachings, we look back at the Old Testament pictures to see the revelations of God's historical provision of a Savior, which was Jesus Christ. In Abel we see God's respect towards Abel's faith in God's promise of a savior and we see God ministered unto Abel so that he had an inward witness that he pleased God. We also see his faith saved him because even though he was dead he was still alive.

> And to Jesus the mediator of the new covenant, and to the blood of sprinkling, that speaketh better things than that of Abel. (Heb. 12:24)

When Cain and Abel presented themselves unto God, they were symbolic of the only two ways man can approach God. Man can come to God his own way or he can come to God in God's way. Abel pleased God by demonstrating his faith in God through the sacrifice of a perfect, innocent, sacrificial lamb. Cain failed to please God by coming to God without faith, as he tried to earn God's respect through his own good works. This is the basic lesson of the Bible, the difference between faith and religion. We can come to God by faith in the Lamb of God, which He has provided, or we can try to cover ourselves and come unto God our own way, which God calls sin. This theme develops throughout the whole Bible, showing the difference between the human having faith in God's heavenly provision or the human trying to please God and earn salvation through their own good works. This principle is the heart of the Bible. God has made provision for the creature and the creature must come to God in God's way. When we trust in the Lamb of God, which He has provided, God covers us with the precious living blood of Jesus. In this way God gives us the life that is eternal through Jesus, the one that has been raised from the dead for us.

> Jesus saith unto him, I am the way, the truth, and the life: no man cometh unto the Father, but by me. (John 14:6)

We see throughout the Old Testament, as the the people came before the priests and confessed their sins while laying their hands upon the lamb, the sins of the human were transferred to the lamb, providing forgiveness to the human. Then the lamb was slain by the priest as the result of sin and its life was lost. After that, the body of the lamb was burned in the fire, the blood of that lamb was then sprinkled upon the mercy seat of the ark in a compartment of the tabernacle called the holy of holies and the life of the human was spared. The blood covered the sins of the human, and the human was forgiven of their sins. This process of transference and forgiveness, through the death of the innocent for the sins of the guilty, was practiced daily. God provided this process as a mental picture for the Israelites as they believed forward in the future that God's Savior would surely come.

> I will say of the LORD, He is my refuge and my fortress: my God; in him will I trust. (Ps. 91:2)

God has promised us eternal life through the death of His only Son as our substitute. If you think you can earn God's respect by your own goodness, then you can't be in God's family. If you can't trust God to keep His promise and meet your every need, then you can't be in God's family. If you can't believe in the provision God has made for you through His only Son, then you can't be in God's family. There is no human born of Adam that has the power to keep himself alive forever. There is no human that has the power to earn God's respect enough for God to grant him eternal life, but God shows His respect towards our faith in Jesus Christ. Jesus is both God and man and He is now our high priest. Jesus is the Lord of Heaven and all those who respect Him as God's Son and by faith receive

Him, as Lord in their lives, will be allowed to know Him as Lord on earth and also in Heaven. The life that is eternal is the lifestyle of walking with the heavenly Father. Jesus will cover you with His righteousness and bring you back to God. Jesus said, "I am the way, the truth and the life. No man comes to the Father *but by me*" (John 4:6)." God covers all by that which has died, through Christ in me.

3. I Only Live By That Which Is Raised

So Abraham took the wood of the burnt offering and laid it on Isaac his son; and he took the fire in his hand, and a knife, and the two of them went together. But Isaac spoke to Abraham his father and said, "My father!" And he said, "Here I am, my son." Then he said, "Look, the fire and the wood, but where is the lamb for a burnt offering?" And Abraham said, "My son, *God will provide* for Himself the lamb for a burnt offering." So the two of them went together. Then they came to the place of which God had told him. And Abraham built an altar there and placed the wood in order; and he bound Isaac his son and laid him on the altar, upon the wood. And Abraham stretched out his hand and took the knife to slay his son. But the Angel of the LORD called to him from heaven and said, "Abraham, Abraham!" So he said, "Here I am." And He said, "Do not lay your hand on the lad, or do anything to him; for now, I know that you fear God, since you have not withheld your son, your only son, from Me." Then Abraham lifted his eyes and looked, and there behind him was a ram caught in a thicket by its horns. So Abraham went and took the ram, and offered it up for a burnt offering instead of his son. And Abraham called the name of the place, The-LORD-Will-Provide; as it is said to this day, "In the Mount of The LORD it shall be provided." Then the Angel of the LORD called to Abraham a second time out of heaven, and said: "By Myself I have sworn, says the LORD, because you have done this thing, and have not withheld your son, your only son-- blessing I will bless you, and multiplying I will multiply your descendants as the stars of the heaven and as the sand which is on the seashore;

and your descendants shall possess the gate of their enemies. In your seed all the nations of the earth shall be blessed, because *you have obeyed My voice.*" (Genesis 22:6-18 NKJV)

The theme of the Lamb continues with Abraham and Isaac. Abraham was a moon worshipper from the land of Ur. God called him out of Ur to walk with Him to fulfill God's purpose. When Abraham obeyed God, he died to his own dreams and plans and began to walk with God. This principle of giving up your natural destiny in obedience to God puts us in position to receive an eternal destiny, which only comes from God. What God offers us is always greater than what we can accomplish with our lives. God calls us the same way, but few will respond. Even though we are worshipping the things that are seen, God calls us to walk with Him in the Spirit all the way to the heavenly city. When we respond to God the way Abraham did, we begin our new destiny where *we only live by that which is raised.* God told Abraham, "by doing what I told you to do you have unlocked the treasures of Heaven for everyone and through your seed will all the families of the earth be blessed."

Through Abraham, God demonstrates to us that He is a Father. God changed his name from Abram, which means father, to Abraham, which means father of many nations. Abraham is the first person who became a different race by faith in God. Even though he was called the father of many nations and it was impossible to have a child in his old age with his old wife, he believed God. This is a picture of our call from God to walk with Him in eternal life, of how we should respond to Him and how we believe in His promises. God promised Abraham, even though it was impossible, he would have a miracle child with Sarah that would bless all the families of the earth. At 100 years old he still didn't have a child, yet he believed God and God called him Abraham, the father of many nations. This is symbolic of God's way of raising us from what we are to what He created us to be. Abraham's faith teaches us that in dying to the old we are raised to walk in newness of life with God. Abraham was called the friend of God. Faith exalts us from the position of being enemies of God to being friends of God.

(As it is written, I have made thee a father of many nations,) before him whom *he believed,* even God, who quickeneth the dead, and calleth those things which be not as though they were. Who *against hope believed in hope*, that he might become the father of many nations, according to that which was spoken, So shall thy seed be. And being *not weak in faith*, he considered not *his own body now dead*, when he was about an hundred years old, neither yet *the deadness of Sara's womb*: He staggered not at the promise of God through unbelief; but was *strong in faith, giving glory to God*; And *being fully persuaded* that, what he had promised, he was able also to perform. And therefore it was imputed to him for righteousness. Now it was not written for his sake alone, that it was imputed to him; But *for us also, to whom it shall be imputed, if we believe* on him that raised up Jesus our Lord from the dead; Who was delivered *for our offences*, and was raised again *for our justification*. (Rom. 4:17-25)

Old Abraham had the miracle child Isaac with his wife Old Sarah who had a barren womb. Isaac was the promised seed of Abraham. Isaac had Jacob, and out of Jacob came the twelve tribes of Israel. Abraham and Sarah had a miracle child when they were over 100 years old. The Bible says in Romans 4:17-25, ". . . and being not weak in faith, Abraham considered not his own body now dead, when he was about a hundred years old, neither yet the deadness of Sarah's womb." So Abraham's body was dead and Sarah's womb was barren. Spiritually they were double dead and it was double impossible, for him and her. Isaac was the son of promise, born by the power of God. Their miracle child points us to the miracle child, Jesus, who would be born of a virgin. In this passage of scripture God calls Isaac "thine only son," even though Abraham also had Ishmael. That is because just as Abraham and Sarah became Jews by faith in the power of God, even so Isaac was born by the power of God and Ishmael was not. God's promises in the Bible teach us to trust in the power of God, not in the arm of the flesh.

And, behold, the word of the LORD came unto him, saying, this shall not be thine heir; but he that shall come forth out of thine own bowels shall be thine heir. (Genesis 15:4)

Abraham and Sarah had tried to help God out and hurry things up. They thought by having a child through their servant Hagar, they would accomplish God's goal but God's goal is never accomplished by unblessed human efforts. All humans go through the process of trying to help God out before fully trusting in God, but that is part of the lesson of the Bible. We cannot accomplish what God wants to do. God doesn't need our help, just our faith. God Himself must make provision for us. He is God and we are not. Our needs can only be met through the power of God. This is symbolic of the fact that what originates with man cannot partake in the spiritual inheritance. Only through what God provides can we partake of the spiritual inheritance. I only live by that which is raised.

> For it is written, that *Abraham had two sons*, the one by a bondmaid, the other by a freewoman. But he who was of the bondwoman was born after the flesh; but he of the freewoman was by promise. Which things are an allegory: for *these are the two covenants*; the one from the mount Sinai, which gendereth to bondage, which is Agar. For this Agar is mount Sinai in Arabia, and answereth to Jerusalem which now is, and is in bondage with her children. But Jerusalem which is above is free, which is the mother of us all. For it is written, Rejoice, thou barren that bearest not; break forth and cry, thou that travailest not: for the desolate hath many more children than she which hath an husband. *Now we, brethren, as Isaac was, are the children of promise. But as then he that was born after the flesh persecuted him that was born after the Spirit, even so it is now.* Nevertheless what saith the scripture? Cast out the bondwoman and her son: for *the son of the bondwoman shall not be heir with the son of the freewoman.* So then, brethren, we are not children of the bondwoman, but of the free. (Gal. 4:22-31)

In Genesis 15, God told Abraham that Ishmael shall not be his heir, but a miracle child shall come forth out of his own bowels and be his heir. In Genesis chapter 22 we see God telling Abraham to take Isaac, thine only son, up to Mount Moriah. Ishmael had been sent away some years earlier. This is by design. This teaches us that we have to put aside the ways of the flesh before we can enjoy walking in the Spirit. Do you remember the original promise God made to Adam and Eve? He said the promised one would come through the seed of the woman (virgin birth). Only the power of God can produce a child in a virgin. Birth and rebirth is a God-thing. In Galatians 4:22-31, God is showing us the two sons represent two births. The first son Ishmael represents the first birth, which the Bible calls the natural man, born of Adam. By earthly tradition the firstborn is the heir. The natural man is flesh and blood and is condemned under the law. The Bible says the natural man cannot inherit the kingdom of God. The second son Isaac represents the second birth, which the Bible calls the spiritual man. He is free from the law and lives under the Grace of God. The spiritual birth is the rebirth of the human spirit. In the eyes of God, he is the true heir. The enmity between the two sons represents the spiritual hostility between the first-born and the second-born, the natural man and the spiritual man. They are fighting over the inheritance. But God is teaching us the true inheritance is spiritual, not natural. It is heavenly, not earthly. The firstborn (our body) lives for the natural inheritance, but the second born (our spirit) lives for the spiritual inheritance. He wants to live by that which is raised.

Know ye not, brethren, (for I speak to them that know the law), how that the law hath dominion over a man as long as he liveth? For the woman which hath an husband is bound by the law to her husband so long as he liveth; but if the husband be dead, she is loosed from the law of her husband. So then if, while her husband liveth, she be married to another man, she shall be called an adulteress: but if her husband be dead, she is free from that law; so that she is no adulteress, though she be married to another man. Wherefore, my brethren, ye also are become dead to the law by the body of Christ; that ye should be married to another, even to Him who is raised from the dead, that we should bring forth fruit unto God. (Rom. 7:1-4)

God uses the marriage covenant to show us how we are married to the nature of the flesh until we die to it and become alive unto the divine nature of the Spirit. Jesus said, *"Ye must be born of the Spirit or you cannot enter the Kingdom of God."* The miracle child Isaac points us to the miracle of the new birth that makes it possible for us to become God's children. God doesn't see us in the natural man as one of His sons. God sees us in the spiritual man as one of His sons. This is part of the secret of eternity and God is trying to teach us this lesson of eternity all the way through the Bible. So even though it was double impossible for Abraham and Sarah to have a son, by faith in God's promise of the power of God, they had the miracle child. This points us to how we become born again by faith in God's promise.

> And he said, Take now thy son, thine only son Isaac, whom thou lovest, and get thee into the land of Moriah; and offer him there for a burnt offering upon one of the mountains which I will tell thee of. (Genesis 22:2)

Then one day God told Abraham to offer up his *miracle child* Isaac as an offering to God upon the mount of Moriah. You can imagine the heartache of Abraham when he realizes his miracle child is going to die. Abraham obeyed God. Abraham's trip to Moriah was three days just like Jesus' trip to Hell lasted three days. Isaac submitted to his father's will just like Jesus submitted to His Father's will. Abraham put the wood on Isaac just like God put the cross on Jesus. The father and his son walked up the mount just like God and His Son walked up the mount. As they were going up the mount to offer a sacrifice unto God, Isaac asked Abraham, "where is the lamb?" One day, God is going to call out to you and He will ask you, "where is your lamb?" What will you say? Abraham said, "My son, God will provide for Himself a Lamb."

Jesus was the promised Son just like Isaac. Jesus was promised to us all. Jesus is the perfect lamb God provided for us. By faith Abraham offered up his only son and by faith Isaac offered himself unto God upon the altar. Isaac was just as tender in his obedience to Abraham his father as Jesus was in His obedience to God His Father. Abraham bound Isaac to the wood just like God bound Jesus to the cross. As Abraham lifted the knife to sacrifice his son Isaac, God called to Abraham out of Heaven, saying, "Hold the knife, Abraham." Then they saw the animal to be sacrificed, being held for them in a *bush of thorns*. As the animal went upon the altar, Isaac came off the altar to walk in a new destiny with God. When we believe in Jesus as our sacrifice, we are given a new eternal destiny to walk in. Father Abraham proved his love for God just like God the Father proved His love by offering up His only Son for us. As Abraham and Isaac stood back and watched the animal sacrifice burning upon Isaac's altar, I believe Isaac realized God's principle of *I only live by that which is raised.*

> And the angel of the LORD called unto him out of heaven, and said, Abraham, Abraham: and he said, Here am I. And he said, Lay not thine hand upon the lad, neither do thou anything unto him: for now I know that thou fearest God, seeing thou hast not withheld thy son, thine only son from me. (Genesis 22:11-12)

God is demonstrating to us through Abraham and Isaac how He made provision for us and how we appropriate the power of God in His provision. The sacrifice was provided when Abraham and Isaac were obedient. The sacrifice was provided when Isaac was willing to lay down his life upon the altar. Jesus said, "He that findeth his life shall lose it: and he that loseth his life for my sake shall find it" (Matt. 10:39). Isaac came off the altar when the sacrifice was provided. When we are willing to lay down our natural man of self upon the altar, in obedience to God like Isaac did, we are learning that we can only live by that which is raised by God for us. God is showing us our dying to self is the trigger of His resurrection power. God offered up His only Son for us just like Abraham did. Just as God provided Abraham with a sacrifice held in a bush of thorns, God provided for us an innocent sacrifice held by a crown of thorns. Jesus laid down His life on the cross for us just like Isaac laid down his life on the altar. Isaac rose up changed, just looking at the sacrifice afar off. Looking at Jesus as our sacrifice afar off changes us. God knows we fear Him when He sees we don't withhold that which He is asking us to sacrifice, which is the offspring of our natural life, the self. As our natural man dies, we only live by that new man, which is raised by the power of God inside our faith filled hearts.

We aren't just getting a ticket to Heaven. We are doing what Abraham did, what Isaac did and what Jesus did. We are laying down our life and taking it up again. The Bible says we must put off mortality and put on immortality. *Something must die that I might live.* Jesus did that for us. Because of Jesus, God now *covers all by that which has died.* Now our part is that by faith, *we only live by that which is raised.* When we give up our earthly life, which we treasure, unto God, like Abraham gave up Isaac, the love of his heart, to God, we are able to see God's promise of provision for us.

When we believe and obey God like Isaac believed and obeyed his father Abraham, we come out of death the same way Isaac came out of death. We see God's provision for us of the substitutionary sacrifice of Jesus afar off upon the cross, and we rise up like Isaac to walk in newness of life, leaving the old life behind. We don't actually die, like Isaac didn't die, but we reckon ourselves dead unto sin and alive unto God through Jesus Christ. We see our death was given to Him and His life is now being given unto us. In this way *we only live by that which is raised.* In this event God is teaching us that as we lay down our earthly life like Isaac and see Christ has died in our place, then we know Christ is alive in us now and we are alive with Him forevermore. God said to Abraham, "Because you have not withheld your only son from me, I have sworn to do the same for you and your seed." What Abraham did in the natural realm with his only son, God did in the spiritual realm with His only Son. The Bible says in Galatians 3, and Hebrews 11, that God preached the gospel unto Abraham and "Abraham believed God would raise Isaac from the dead." Jesus said to the Jews, "Abraham saw my day and was glad."

> By faith Abraham, when he was tried, offered up Isaac: and he that had received the promises offered up his only begotten son, Of whom it was said, That in Isaac shall thy seed be called: Accounting that God was able to raise him up, even from the dead; from whence also he received him in a figure. (Heb. 11:17-19)

I believe Abraham saw (by revelation) God sacrificing His only Son there upon that mount, centuries before Jesus came, prophesying the same. It was upon the same Mount Moriah where Abraham offered Isaac up to God, which we call Calvary, that Jesus was historically crucified. If you look at the cross of Jesus upon the mount, God's provision of the Lamb of God can be seen. Can you see God showing you His pictures in the Old Testament? Can you see how God uses them to point us to the one person that can save us from the powers of death? Do you now understand why Jesus is *the Only Son* of God and how we can only live by that which is raised? Other religions want to include the founders of their religions, but God said the last Adam, Jesus Christ, is God's only Son. The life that is eternal, that operates by the power of God and that overcomes death, comes to us *through God's Only Son*. God historically raised Jesus from the dead and His resurrection is the climax of history. The empty tomb puts all others to silence. God has historically shown us the truth that in Christ, we only live by that which is raised.

> For it became him, for whom are all things, and by whom are all things, in bringing many sons unto glory, to make the captain of their salvation perfect through sufferings. (Heb. 2:10)

God is having His family and He is bringing many sons unto glory. Every human is born with the call of God to enter into fellowship with the Creator, come to know Him as Father, and become a child of God. That was God's original intention and nothing has changed. The God of Heaven has created every human with the call of son-ship. God had one Son and He wanted many more. He created the universe to give man a place to live and then He created man for His purpose of having a family. We are all called to be a part of God's eternal family. He is the author of our salvation. He is the pattern of eternal life and through His suffering, He has perfectly authored for us the way to become the sons of God.

> And so it is written, The first man Adam was made *a living soul*; the last Adam was made *a quickening spirit*. (1 Cor. 15:45)

Herein is the solution God has provided for every soul ever born. God has sent us the last Adam, which is Jesus Christ. The Bible says the first Adam was a living soul, but the last Adam is a quickening Spirit. All humans born of Adam are born as living souls, but Jesus wasn't born of Adam. Jesus was the Son of God, born into earth as the seed of the woman. The very fact He was born of a virgin proves He is a quickening spirit, because God is His Father. Only the Spirit of God could provide a body for Jesus in the womb of a virgin without the blood of the human sperm, which passes down the corrupt nature of Adam. The woman provides the egg, which becomes the body of the human. The man provides the sperm, which makes the egg alive and determines the blood of the human.

The Bible says over and over, "The life of the flesh is in the blood." Jesus didn't have the corrupted blood of Adam through a human father to bring Him into the world like you and me. God was His Father. So God quickened Mary and formed in her the body of Jesus. The blood of Jesus was living blood without any sin in it. His lifestyle of walking with God was a living demonstration of the divine nature, which He wants to give us. In the next few chapters you will see what happened from the cross to the throne and be able to understand how Jesus is the Savior of the world.

Because of Jesus we now have the same choice and opportunity Adam had to put on immortality. Will you continue to eat only from the Tree of Knowledge or will you eat of the Tree of Life and be quickened and transformed by the knowledge that comes through the words of God? The contrasts between the two are like the east from the west. Knowledge alone doesn't impart life. The Knowledge of God through the words of God imparts eternal life. Even though we are dead and are going to die, God has provided us with life, through Jesus Christ. When it is time to die, knowledge alone won't save you. Your faith in the goodness of God will save you. Now you know why Jesus had to come from Heaven and be born of a virgin and why Jesus had to die on a dead tree called the cross.

I have said everything in the first few chapters to set you up for the last three chapters. I've brought you along slowly to help you develop a focus of faith.

So far you have learned,

- ✔ How God quickens our hearts by His words
- ✔ How to prepare your heart
- ✔ The human has a problem called death
- ✔ The death problem is impossible for man to fix
- ✔ Only God has the solution to man's death problem
- ✔ God's solution to man's death problem is called life
- ✔ What sin is, what self is
- ✔ What death is, what life is
- ✔ Something must die that I might live
- ✔ God covers all by that which has died
- ✔ I only live by that which is raised
- ✔ God has made provision for us through His Son, Jesus

By now you should be strong enough to see the power of God the Bible wants to release into you. In the first few chapters, I've given you milk and now I'm going to give you some meat. The next few chapters will narrow the focus of the Bible down to three main points. They are as follows:

- ✔ Your sins are gone.
- ✔ You must be born again.
- ✔ You can be a son.

If you will focus on these three main phases of spiritual things, you should be able to easily understand the Bible and take advantage of the goodness of God and the power of God.

Personal Study Notes

CHAPTER 6

YOUR SINS *Are* GONE

To wit, that God was in Christ, reconciling the world
unto himself, not imputing their trespasses unto them.

2 COR.5:19

God's Oath To Us

> And he said unto them, Ye will surely say unto me this proverb, Physician, heal thyself: whatsoever we have heard done in Capernaum, do also here in thy country. (Luke 4:23)

J esus is called the Great Physician. If you can agree with Jesus that you are spiritually sick, then He can help you. Jesus heals everyone who comes to Him with all their heart. He is no respecter of persons. His program of redemption, restoration and re-creation works for everyone who believes in Him. Jesus did what He did on the cross to make the power of God available to you, because He loves you. Just like a good doctor works to remove cancer, God knew what kind of surgery we needed. You see God talking about His operation all through the Old Testament. The writers of the New Testament show us how God has performed His supernatural operation through Jesus Christ at the cross. What we think is supernatural in this world isn't supernatural. The cross was God's operating table. What God did on the cross was supernatural. That is why Jesus had to die on the cross. God and His Son were working together to destroy Satan's power of death over the human. God did supernatural surgery upon the human race, making it possible for all who believe in Jesus to escape from the power of sin and death.

> And Jesus answering said unto them, they that are whole need not a physician; but they that are sick. (Luke 5:31)

You can see God and His Son working together, doing surgery to remove the cancer of sin and death, from the human, spirit, soul, and body. You can see the human being made whole by God's power. God and His Son were putting death to death. This is the first stage of the secret of eternity, which was kept secret but is now being made manifest to all believers. Satan had put man to death in the first Adam and God provided us with the last Adam, to take us out of death and into life. God is a good Creator and He had always purposed for man to have His eternal life. Death was never a part of God's original plan. Death is an enemy of God and man. God is better than any human physician. He is the Great Physician and has accomplished the defeat of death for us. Do you have faith in the operation of God?

For men verily swear by the greater: and an oath for confirmation is to them an end of all strife. Wherein God, willing more abundantly to shew unto the heirs of promise the immutability of his counsel, confirmed it by an oath: That by two immutable things, in which it was impossible for God to lie, we might have a strong consolation, who have fled for refuge to lay hold upon the hope set before us: Which hope we have as an anchor of the soul, both sure and sted-fast, and which entereth into that within the veil. (Heb. 6:16-19)

The Hippocratic oath that doctors recite originated in Greece around the fifth century BC. Most believe Hippocrates, who is considered to be the father of medicine, wrote the oath. Physicians are required to swear by the oath to uphold specific ethical standards. The oath is sort of a rite of passage for those who *practice* medicine. God did even better. Not only did God promise before creation to give us eternal life, but the Bible says He even swore an oath by Himself, because He could swear by no greater, to bring us back into life. He did this by coming in the likeness of sinful flesh (a human body) in order to take the sinful nature of the serpent that was in man to the cross. There He put sin to death and we were made alive in Him. The Greek medical symbol is a serpent upon a pole. Even the physician's symbol points us to the cross where God did supernatural surgery and took the nature of the serpent out of man and put the divine nature of His dear Son into man. God is the Great Physician. God swore to us an oath to do it. We had death in our blood and He gave us a blood transfusion with the blood of Christ. You would do the same for your kids if they were dying and they could be saved by a blood transfusion. The heavenly Father is greater than any human father.

Death and Life

What do you think the requirements are for going to Heaven? If you were to die tonight and you stood before God, and He asked you, "Why should I let you into my Heaven," what would you say? Would you say, "I tried to live a good life," or "I tried to be good all my life," or "I was a good person," or "my good deeds outweighed my bad deeds?"

Before you read any further, please take a minute and just focus on what your answer would be. Religion will not save you. Religion can't save the human just like politics can't save the politician. Neither can politicians save the world. Good works, good deeds, going to church, taking communion, being water baptized, giving money, worshipping idols, saying the rosary, and many other things that men are trusting in won't save you. Religion provides many opportunities for man to appease his conscience, but the Bible solution to our human problem of death isn't designed to make us feel better, but to help us overcome death. God had to save us from the powers of death and from our bondage to the world system, just like He had to save Israel from the death angel and from their bondage to Egypt. There is no earthly solution for our death problem. Only God can save us from the powers of death.

God had nothing to do with death's dominion over man. Death is an enemy of God and man. God examined everything He did during creation and He stood back and observed His work and was satisfied, saying it was good. After creation we see man in the Garden of Eden walking with God in innocence and it was perfectly normal for man to fellowship with God. In fact, walking with God was Paradise for Adam and Eve. They didn't even know they were naked because they were clothed in the light of the glory of God. After they disobeyed God's instructions, they fell out of fellowship with God and joined Satan's be your own god new-world-order bandwagon, their eyes were opened and they knew that they were naked before God of the glory with which God had clothed them.

God was not caught off-guard when Adam rebelled and walked away from Him with the whole human race in his loins. The Bible says God knows the end from the beginning and He knew what Adam would do. The Bible teaches us God and Jesus had planned everything before creation. God and His Son worked together during creation, they worked together during His passion in Israel and they are still working together to prepare a people and a family for Heaven. Is it easier for you to have more faith in the politicians when they make promises to build a better world or to believe in God's program of developing an eternal family through Jesus Christ? God's program is the most practical plan a real loving God could have. God knows how things will end before they begin and His plans always succeed. What God promises, He fulfills.

And he said unto them, Ye are from beneath; I am from above: ye are of this world; I am not of this world. (John 8:23)

Jesus is not of this world. He is from above. We are of this world and in order for us to go from this world into Jesus' world we must go through the change that makes us fit for Heaven. This change takes place as we believe in Jesus Christ. Jesus constantly told everyone that He came from Heaven, that He was sent to earth by His heavenly Father, that He came to do the will of the Father, to give His life as a ransom for us and to destroy Satan's power of death over us. Because of Jesus we are all invited to Heaven and as believers, we should love others as He loved us. They said, "Jesus spoke like never a man spoke" and "He does everything with authority." The Pharisees knew God was with Jesus. We see this fact in the statement of the Pharisee Nicodemus. He said to Jesus in John 3:2, "Rabbi, we know that thou art a teacher come from God, for no man can do these miracles that you are doing, except God be with him."

Search the scriptures; for in them ye think ye have eternal life: and they are they which testify of me. (John 5:39)

Many people have a problem believing Jesus was the Son of God just like they may have problems believing there were once dinosaurs, but Jesus said He was the Son of God and that He came to conquer death for us. No man in history has ever spoken like that. Jesus constantly talked about how He was going to destroy the powers of death over man. Only a savior can talk like that. Jesus believed what the Bible said about Him and He constantly said scripture cannot lie, scripture cannot be broken, and the scriptures must be fulfilled, because the scriptures were about Him.

God Has Forgiven All Your Sins

Have you ever thought about the fact that God has not only forgiven your sins but He has forgiven you of your sins forever? Understanding that alone will affect your life. What do I mean by the word sins? I mean everything you've ever done wrong, every wrong attitude, every mistake, every evil deed, every way of being selfish, and living life without God, past, present and future. God has forgiven you of everything that is offensive to Him.

Notice I said our sins are gone. The Bible says, "All have sinned." That is true of the celebrity, the billionaire, the sex addict, the atheist who doesn't believe and the Christian who isn't perfect. It's true of everyone. Nobody's perfect. All have sinned and come short of earning the glory of fellowship with God. What God does for one, He does for all. Whether you are rich or poor, young or old, a bad person or a good person, no matter what culture or class or vocation, God has loved us so much that He has forgiven us of our sins.

Did you know that God has forgiven you of your sins? How incredible is that? It's true. Again everyone who has ever been born and ever will be born has been forgiven of their sins, through the shed blood of Jesus, which we will talk about shortly. That's part of the good news of the Bible. God so loved you and me that He gave up His only Son, Jesus, to make it possible for you to be forgiven of your sins. God had to forgive you of all your sins before you could go to Heaven. He did this before you were born. According to the Bible you are now forgiven of every sin you've ever committed. How does it feel to hear that? Does it make you feel better? Do you feel forgiven? Do you think that's worth your time to think about or to find out more?

Before you read any further I want you to stop what you are doing and for two minutes I want you to just think about this one thing; God has forgiven you of all your sins.

> To him give all the prophets' witness that through his name whosoever believeth in him shall receive remission of sins. (Acts 10:43)

It sounds almost like a riddle, doesn't it? It's just too good to be true, isn't it? Now I didn't say everyone in the world has received God's gift of the forgiveness of sins. The other side of the riddle is this, whosoever believes in Him shall receive God's gift of forgiveness. That is what this passage of scripture says. Without Jesus, there is no other way to be forgiven of your sins. Without believing in Jesus, there is no other way to receive the forgiveness of all your sins. The Scripture says, if you will believe in Him you will receive the remission of all your sins.

Truth has two sides and they are both razor sharp. There is God's side and man's side. Our side is the death side and God's side is the life side. We can use marriage as an example. When someone says, "I want to marry you," one side is done. He is now marry-able. But the marriage doesn't happen until the other side becomes marry-able. The message of the Bible is like that. God has done His part and now you must do your part for God's gift to be activated in your heart.

The prophets of the Old Testament all point us to the provision of God being the remission of our sins. In the Bible, the word "remission" is far better than "forgiveness." The word remission means pardon and freedom as though sin never existed. It is a judicial word, which means that someone has paid your penalty and you have been declared innocent, as though you never sinned.

> For God so loved the world, that he gave his only begotten Son, that whosoever believeth in him should not perish, but have everlasting life. (John 3:16)

Through Jesus, God has reconciled the world unto Himself. That means God has acquitted you. God sees you as innocent and has declared you not guilty in His sight. The Bible says if you will believe this, you *should not* perish, but have everlasting life. How do we receive God's forgiveness and remission of our sins? The Bible tells us we receive our heavenly pardon by believing the truth.

For you atheists out there who won't believe the Bible because you feel you can't find a Christian who can live what the Bible teaches, I have some news for you. Nobody can live a perfect life. You can't make your kids live a perfect life but you demand it from a Christian. We deceive ourselves into thinking the Bible demands perfection and that can't be accomplished. The Bible teaches that perfection is impossible for the natural man and no human being can perfectly keep the standards of Jesus Christ. If you think your morality is honest then just think again with this thought: can you do any better? No you can't! God doesn't demand perfection. In fact, God doesn't demand anything. God offers us His gift and He encourages us to accept His gift. Through the Bible, God politely tells us He has made provision for us so we can live and not die and He has done so through His only Son, Jesus Christ. Then God politely tells us that all we have to do is believe this good news and it will be activated in our hearts and if we continue in the word of God we will know the truth and the truth will make us free. How easy to believe is that?

All we have to do is believe the truth and trust in the goodness of God. When God sees faith in our hearts, He declares us not guilty in His sight. Our faith in the words of God cleanses us before God. That doesn't make us perfect but it makes us right with God and fit for Heaven. That is too easy for some, but, friend, Jesus did everything for you. Jesus died for you. Jesus was buried for you. Jesus went to Hell for you and Jesus rose again for you. Jesus did it all for you. If you will believe what the Bible says, the power of God will quicken you and you will be born again of the Spirit of God and you will know the Bible teaches the truth of eternity. First God cleans us up, then He fills us up and then He grows us up. It isn't science of the mind but faith in your heart that saves you.

Jesus said, "Except you become as a little child you will not enter the Kingdom of Heaven." You must believe God like your little child believes you or you can't become God's little child and come to know God as your heavenly Father. After that, God doesn't expect perfection, but maturity. Just as in the natural, we expect babes to become children and grow up into adults, even so it is in the spiritual. Spiritual birth is the rebirth of the human spirit and just like it is in the natural so it is in the spiritual. The Spirit of God lights the candle of our human spirit with His Spirit, giving us *new life,* and then we walk with God in life and mature as the light of truth shines into our hearts.

Heaven isn't earned. Heaven is freely given to all believers. As believers mature, they learn to walk with God and as they do they begin to resemble Jesus. We believe ourselves into Christ and we believe ourselves into fellowship with God. No human being can do this perfectly. But we can believe the truth and bear witness to the truth as the truth manifests in our lives.

From the Bible perspective there is no such thing as an atheist. The Bible calls you an unbeliever or a believer, a sinner or a saint. There are good and evil sinners and there are righteous and unrighteous saints, but the truth is the same for us all. Our response to the truth of the Bible is either believer or unbeliever. If you believe then you receive but if you don't believe then you won't receive. God's promise is activated in your heart as you believe. Without faith we are dead to God.

> We then, as workers together with him, beseech you also that ye receive not the grace of God in vain. (2 Cor. 6:1)

Let's say I meet you for the first time and I tell you I have a gift for you. If you believe me, you will expect to receive my gift. But if you won't believe my words that I have a gift for you, then you will just walk away and think I'm crazy. Any time you receive a gift you receive the giver of the gift. If someone gives you a gift, but you refuse to receive it because you don't like that person, then you fail to receive the gift and the giver of the gift. God has done great and mighty things for you through His Son. God has forgiven you of all your sins to make it possible to give you His gift of eternal life. Your sins are gone as far as God is concerned. However, people don't go to Heaven just because God forgave them of their sins. Many false doctrines have come out of that thought. Heaven is a prepared place for a prepared people. Heaven is God's home and the home of His eternal family. The grace of God is the goodness of God and it is beyond our imaginations. God is so good it is almost impossible to believe but faith is what activates the grace of God towards you. God said you will receive all His goodness by believing the truth and He encourages you to not receive the grace of God in vain. There is no pretending with God. He knows whether you are serious about receiving Him or not. You can't receive God's gift without receiving Him. They go together. If you try to receive God's gift apart from receiving God, then you deceive yourself and the truth is not in you. What is your response to that? Have you believed God's testimony about His Son Jesus who paid a very high price for you to have the forgiveness of all your sins?

> Seek ye the LORD while he may be found, call ye upon him while he is near: Let the wicked forsake his way, and the unrighteous man his thoughts: and let him return unto the LORD, and he will have mercy upon him; and to our God, for he will abundantly pardon. (Isa. 55:6-7)

Even though we are forgiven of our sins, we are born rebels and rebels aren't allowed into Heaven. It would be unrighteous of God to just grant full pardon and allow rebels into Heaven. It seems like a paradox, doesn't it? It's sort of like that question, what came first, the chicken or the egg? God wants everyone to come to Heaven, God has invited everyone to Heaven and God has made it possible for everyone to go to Heaven, by forgiving their sins. However, we must receive God's pardon by faith. God has not only forgiven our sins but He has remitted our sins and eternal pardon belongs to us. If we will receive God's gift of reconciliation, He will treat us as innocent of all wrong doing forever. All He asks is that we seek Him while we still have time and call upon Him, forsake our wickedness of living life without Him and thinking like the world thinks. As we return in our hearts to Him, He will have mercy upon us and death itself will not be able to prevail against the mercy of the living God. That is abundant pardon.

> For *by grace* are ye saved *through faith*; and that not of yourselves: it is the gift of God. (Eph. 2:8)

When we believe in the goodness of God, we instantaneously receive the gift of God and it's eternal. It's not just the grace of God that saves us forever. It's not just our faith that saves us forever. It is *by* grace (the goodness of God) *through* our faith that we are saved. It is the gift of God for eternity. What God does is eternal. God has called every soul to become partakers of His divine nature and come to Heaven, but not all will change their attitudes and respond to God. Some will prefer their lot in this world rather than joining God in His world. God has made eternal provision for every soul but He respects everyone's choice. God, in His wisdom, has prepared a place for all those who refuse the goodness of God and don't want to have any part in God's program. That place the Bible calls Hell.

> In this the children of God are manifest, and the children of the devil: whosoever doeth not righteousness is not of God, neither he that loveth not his brother. (1 John 3:10)

In this passage of scripture, we see two spiritual families. When we go through the change of heart, we change spiritual families and as we get into the word of God, our minds begin to change towards a complete transformation of the soul. Faith in God takes us out of the devil's family and transplants us into the family of God. The realities of Heaven and Hell aren't something that the human mind likes to think about, but the Bible says to be spiritually minded is life and peace (see Rom. 8:6). For most people our main concerns every day are going to work to make a living and coming home to our families. Heaven and Hell are the last things on our minds. Hell is such a terror that it is the last thing we want to think about in life. We all tend to think we aren't bad enough to wind up in Hell. Yet the Bible says many will wind up in Hell and few will wind up in Heaven. We want to do anything but think about Hell. The Bible talks about Hell a lot. Heaven and Hell are very real places that affect everyone. I told you this book would challenge you. I also told you this book would comfort you and encourage you.

Right now I want to challenge you to spend a few minutes thinking about Hell. Jesus talked about Hell a lot to the Pharisees. If you take a minute to think about Hell, it may be the most valuable time you've ever spent and could result in the best decision you will ever make. At some point in your life you are going to make a decision that will determine whether you will go there or not. Your decision will be, "Do I want to know God and believe God or not?" That decision will determine your eternal destiny. God doesn't want any human being to go to Hell, but if you don't want to know God, you won't be happy in Heaven.

Hell wasn't created for man but for the devil and his fallen angels. It is also the home of all the devil's children. Man has no business going to Hell. God doesn't want one human to go to Hell. God has dealt with our sins through Jesus Christ and He expects to see you in Heaven. Jesus did all that He did to prevent humans from going to Hell. Jesus paid the price for every soul born of Adam to be saved from Hell. Yet the Bible says many will go to Hell and few will go to Heaven (see Matt. 7:14). Just like God's children will spend eternity with their heavenly Father, even so the children of the devil will spend eternity with their spiritual father, in the place prepared for them called Hell.

The issue is this, Hell is no longer a matter of birth because of Adam, but it is a matter of choice because of Jesus. The moment one believes in Jesus, the Bible says they are born again of His divine nature and they become a citizen of Heaven forever. Did you know that every person in Hell was forgiven of their sins? Did you know that not one person has ever gone to Hell because they were a bad person? Did you know that not one person has ever gone to Heaven because they were a good person? It's true. God's invitation to Heaven can't be earned nor is there anyone on earth that deserves it. Martin Luther once said, "Good works doesn't make a man good, but a good man does good works." Even so, bad deeds don't make a man bad, but a bad man does bad deeds. So bad deeds aren't what send a person to Hell and good deeds aren't what send a person to Heaven. Got it?

The saddest thing in the universe, *in my opinion,* is everyone in Hell today realizes they went there needlessly, that they ought not be in Hell, and that Jesus paid the price for them to escape Hell and come to Heaven. I think everyone in Hell knows the truth and now they realize they are going to be there, suffering the punishment of Hell forever even though the price was already paid by Jesus for us to enjoy the glories of Heaven forever. They know they ought not to be in Hell. And now they will be separated from God and suffering the punishment of Hell forever, even though the price of their redemption was already paid. Can you imagine a greater paradox? But they didn't activate the gift of God. They didn't believe in God's word and allow God to do His work. Faith in the testimony of God is the only way His power can be activated in our hearts. They didn't repent of living life without God and they didn't receive God's provision of the remission of their sins, through the Son of God, the one who took away their sin problem.

> And whosoever shall exalt himself shall be abased; and he that shall humble himself shall be exalted. (Matt. 23:12)

But you don't have to go there. God doesn't want you to go there. God sent Jesus there to make it possible for you to not go there. The Bible calls upon all human beings to humble themselves before God so they can believe the truth and be saved and have eternal life. If you can humble yourself, you can come to know God personally and become a citizen of Heaven, but if you can't humble yourself, you don't belong in Heaven. God only exalts those who are willing to humble themselves. Hopefully this book is making some things clear so you can make a wise decision.

> Humble yourselves therefore under the mighty hand of God, that he may exalt you in due time. (1 Pet. 5:6)

Through Jesus Our Passover Lamb

Then Moses called for all the elders of Israel and said to them, "Pick out and take lambs for yourselves according to your families, and kill the Passover lamb. And you shall take a bunch of hyssop, dip it in the blood that is in the basin, and strike the lintel and the two doorposts with the blood that is in the basin. And none of you shall go out of the door of his house until morning. For the LORD will pass through to strike the Egyptians; and when He sees the blood on the lintel and on the two doorposts, the LORD will pass over the door and not allow the destroyer to come into your houses to strike you. And you shall observe this thing as an ordinance for you and your sons forever. It will come to pass when you come to the land, which the LORD will give you, just as He promised, that you shall keep this service. And it shall be, when your children say to you, 'What do you mean by this service?' that you shall say, 'It is the Passover sacrifice of the LORD, who passed over the houses of the children of Israel in Egypt when He struck the Egyptians and delivered our households. So the people bowed their heads and worshiped. Then the children of Israel went away and did so; just as the LORD had commanded Moses and Aaron, so they did. (Exod. 12:21-28)

God continues showing us the theme of the Lamb and the blood of the Lamb through the Old Testament pictures with Moses. He is the picture of our coming deliverer, Jesus Christ, who is also our Passover Lamb. The law of earth is *thou shalt surely die.* The death angel was going to pass through Egypt to smite the firstborn of Egypt. In this event, Egypt under the rule of Pharaoh, enforcing the bondage of slavery over the people of Israel, represents the world system under the dominion of Satan that enslaves man under the dominion of death. The firstborn of Egypt represents the principle that the natural human, born of the earth, under bondage to this world system, will surely die. The death angel comes to all of the firstborn. The people of Israel are the children of Abraham. They are God's people and God provided Moses as their deliverer. God calls Israel His first-born. They represent unto us the spiritual principle that God is having a family. But the phrase "the first-born" always suggests a second-born, pointing us to the New Birth. With Moses, God demonstrates to us how He has provided Jesus as our deliverer from the powers of death, making it possible for us to be born again into God's family. The second-born are those that are born again of God's Spirit. God calls them *His first-born*. God uses Israel as the picture to us of His first-born. The heavenly law of the Bible is "God makes provision for His people." Those who believe God's word are born of God's Spirit and have been made alive unto God to become His people. God's provision was the innocent sacrificial Passover Lamb.

With the death angel, we see all the firstborn of Egypt without the heavenly provision would die, but the firstborn of Israel, with God's provision, would live (be passed over by the death angel). What was the heavenly provision? It was a perfect lamb without spot and the shed blood of the lamb upon the doors of their homes. God is giving us another view of how the guilty sinner can come to God through His Son and be saved.

God instructed them through Moses to fellowship with their perfect lamb without spot for several days and then kill it. The lamb without spot represented Jesus, the perfect man. Then they were to put the blood of the lamb on the door of their house in the shape of a cross and then shut the door and eat the lamb inside the house as the death angel passed over them. This event was called the Passover. This picture represents to us our need for two things, a perfect lamb and the blood of that lamb. God is teaching us that when we come to Him with our perfect lamb (Jesus) and the blood of His Lamb is upon the door (our hearts) of our house (our bodies), the death angel passes over us. When the death angel came through the camp and saw the blood on the doors of the homes of God's people, he saw that someone had died so he passed over them because the death had already been accomplished in those families where he saw the perfect innocent blood. The firstborn of Egypt is the natural human. He has to die. His blood has to leave his body to end the cycle of the sin nature. When his blood is shed, and he is dead, that is the end of that life. The lambs that were killed represented the innocent sacrificial Lamb of God that would come, shed His blood and die for us.

Then they also had to roast the lamb. This is symbolic of the Lamb of God going into the fires of Hell for us. They were to eat the flesh of the perfect lamb that died for them. This example signifies our union with Christ and with the body of Christ as we feed upon the knowledge of God in Christ Jesus. While the blood of the lamb was on the outside of their house, each person of the family inside the house was instructed to eat the roasted lamb for himself, as the death angel passed over. Eating the perfect lamb that was roasted in the fire, behind the door that was covered with blood, signifies the blood that was shed covered them, the perfect lamb was inside them and that God's provision had the power to save them. This historical event called the Passover is another Bible clue to us that anyone who believes in Jesus, and has the blood of God's Lamb over the door of their hearts, has Jesus inside them and they will be saved. Those who don't love Jesus in their hearts and accept Him as their Lamb and His innocent blood as their payment for sin will not escape the powers of death.

> And if ye call on the Father, who without respect of persons judgeth according to every man's work, pass the time of your sojourning here in fear: Forasmuch as ye know that ye were not redeemed with corruptible things, as silver and gold, from your vain conversation received by tradition from your fathers; But with the precious blood of Christ, as of a lamb without blemish and without spot. (1 Pet. 1:17-19)

God has made provision for every human being, but few will activate and apply God's provision that entitles them to God's gift of eternal life and citizenship in God's heavenly family. God says the only way you can come to Him is with your perfect, innocent, sacrificial Lamb of God. That Lamb of God that shed His blood for you so you could live is God's first-born Son, Jesus Christ.

God Has Reconciled Us unto Himself

> For I will be merciful to their unrighteousness, and their sins and their iniquities will I remember no more. (Heb. 8:12)

> And their sins and iniquities will I remember no more. (Heb. 10:17)

Soon after the nails were in His hands, Jesus prayed for them, saying, "Father forgive them for they know not what they do." Jesus voluntarily became the Lamb of God for us so God could put away our sins. Because of Jesus we can be forgiven of every sin we've ever committed. Friend, if God can forgive those who nailed the nails into the hands of the Son of God, He can forgive you. The only sin God will not forgive is the sin of unbelief. If we refuse to believe in the goodness of God through His only Son, then we stand condemned before God of rejecting His heavenly provision and we are unfit for Heaven. God wants to see us in Heaven but we decide whether or not we arrive at the final destination of the city of God. God's mercy has triumphed over God's judgment. If you refuse His mercy, you stand guilty under God's judgment. As far as God is concerned He remembers your sins *no more*. He has reconciled you unto Himself and He is waiting for you to do your part and become reconciled unto Him.

> To wit, that *God was in Christ, reconciling the world unto himself*, not imputing their trespasses unto them; and hath committed unto us the word of reconciliation. Now then we are ambassadors for Christ, as though God did beseech you by us: we pray you in Christ's stead, *be ye reconciled to God*. For he hath made him to be sin for us, who knew no sin; that we might be made the righteousness of God in him. (2 Cor. 5:19-21)

In these passages of scripture, we see God was in Christ upon the cross. The Bible says that God was in Christ reconciling the world unto Himself, not holding against men their trespasses, but canceling them. This is the main thing God wants us to know that was going on in Jesus Christ. This is what God was saying to His people all through the Old Testament. They all were looking forward to the day that God would send the Savior that He had promised He would send. All through the Old Testament men came to God with their innocent sacrificial lambs and God would forgive their sins as they had faith in God's mercy toward them through the substitution of a living creature dying in their stead. This type of faith looked forward to the day when God would send His Son from Heaven to die for us that we might be reconciled unto God.

Now it was not written for his sake alone, that it was imputed to him; But for us also, to whom it shall be imputed, if we believe on him that raised up Jesus our Lord from the dead; Who was *delivered for our offences*, and *was raised again for our justification*. (Rom. 4:23-25)

This is where God did what no religion can do. God provided a Savior who has conquered death for us and has taken our punishment for sin. Since the historical resurrection of Jesus, we look back in faith to see what God has done for us through Jesus Christ. Just like anything else becomes real to us when we believe it, even so when we have faith in what God says He has done, God's own Spirit quickens us and makes it real to us. God was in Christ and God has already dealt with everything that belonged to us. God says, He will remember our sins no more forever.

He that believeth on the Son hath everlasting life: and he that believeth not the Son shall not see life; but the wrath of God abideth on him. (John 3:3)

Here is the good news of the Bible: your sins are gone. God isn't holding one sin against you. God isn't angry with anyone anymore. God poured out His entire wrath toward us upon Jesus. God has dealt with the sin issue. God has given His word that He will not remember our sins. God has no interest in holding your sins against you. The Bible says God has reconciled the whole human race unto Himself and He has forgiven every soul of their sins, past, present, and future. According to the Bible, God has made provision for every soul. The question everyone should ask is, if God has forgiven me of all my sins and isn't angry with me, am I going to Heaven? The answer to that question is, do you have your Lamb? If you come to God without the Lamb, then the Bible says in John 3:36, the wrath of God abides on you. If you come to God with your innocent sacrificial Lamb of God with faith in your heart, the Bible says, when we were justified (declared righteous) He was raised. God now calls you righteous in His sight and nothing shall separate you from the love of God in Christ Jesus.

Your Sins Are Gone

> Whom God hath set forth to be a propitiation through faith in his
> blood, to declare his righteousness for the remission of sins that are
> past, through the forbearance of God. (Rom. 3:25)

Does it shock you to hear in the Bible that God has forgiven and remitted
everyone's sins and all one has to do to become a citizen of Heaven is to
believe in Jesus and receive His heavenly provision? It's true. Forgiveness
of sins belongs to every person who has ever been born of Adam. But have
you come to God with faith in your heart and received forgiveness of sins?

> The next day John seeth Jesus coming unto him, and saith, Be-
> hold the Lamb of God, which taketh away the sin of the world.
> (John 1:29)

Just as God reckoned everything Adam did unto us when we were in
Adam, even so God has reckoned everything Jesus did unto us who are
believers in Christ. Forgiveness of sins belongs to you. The Bible says the
Lamb of God took away the sins of the world. Jesus paid the price for every
soul born of Adam to be forgiven of their sins. God only asks us to believe
in His Son, the last Adam. That's why the Bible is called the Good News.
You are forgiven of every sin you've ever committed. In Christ, God treats
us as though we've never sinned.

> And without controversy great is the mystery of godliness: God was
> manifest in the flesh, justified in the Spirit, seen of angels, preached
> unto the Gentiles, believed on in the world, received up into glory.
> (1 Tim. 3:16)

Everything Jesus did He did for us. Jesus left Heaven and came to earth
to become our substitute. This is the theme of the Bible from the beginning
to the end. God has made a way for us to escape from the powers of death.
Jesus is the way. He is our sacrificial lamb and He is our high priest who
brings us back to God. Have you received God's heavenly provision for you
of the perfect innocent sacrificial Lamb of God?

To him give all the prophets witness, that through his name whosoever believeth in him shall receive remission of sins. (Acts 10:43)

Do you know what the difference between forgiveness and remission
is? Forgiveness is what happened in the Old Testament when the people
laid their hands on the innocent sacrificial lamb and as the people confessed their sins before the priests, their sins were transferred to the lamb.
This process removed from them their guilt of sin but it didn't remove
their sin nature, so they had to make sacrifices regularly. Then the lamb
was slain by the priest, the body of the lamb was burned in the fire, the
blood of the lamb was sprinkled upon the mercy seat, and their sins were
covered, until next time. All these things were symbolic examples of what
God would one day accomplish through Jesus Christ, but their sins were
only covered; their sin nature remained and there was still a remembrance
of sin. However, watching an innocent creature suffer and die in their
place helped them to believe the judgment of their sin was gone.

And that repentance and remission of sins should be preached in
his name among all nations, beginning at Jerusalem. (Luke 24:47)

The Law of God constantly taught the knowledge of sin. But through
the sacrifice of Jesus we receive the remission of sins. This means our
sins are not only forgiven, but they are removed and even though we
have all sinned, God treats us as though we never sinned because Jesus
bore our sins for us. Everyone who has ever gone to Hell went there with
their sins forgiven, but they failed to receive Jesus the one who provided
the remission of their sins. As the Lamb of God, Jesus not only takes
our sins and our sin nature away from us but He also gives us His divine
nature. When we come to God and become born again of God's Spirit,
we become new creatures in Christ Jesus and God looks at us and sees no
sin. Through our faith in the blood of Jesus, God declares us righteous
in His sight.

Then Peter said unto them, Repent, and be baptized every one of
you in the name of Jesus Christ for the remission of sins, and ye
shall receive the gift of the Holy Ghost. (Acts 2:38)

You know you don't have to go to Hell. You are still in the flesh and you can believe God and come to know God for yourself. Is it clear enough that God wants you in Heaven? If God so loved you that He gave up His only begotten Son so that you don't have to go to Hell, so you can put on immortality and go to Heaven, you ought to realize how much He loves you and how much He wants you in Heaven.

> Grace and peace be multiplied unto you through the knowledge of God, and of Jesus our Lord, According as his divine power hath given unto us all things that pertain unto life and godliness, through the knowledge of him that hath called us to glory and virtue: Whereby are given unto us exceeding great and precious promises: that by these ye might be partakers of the divine nature, having escaped the corruption that is in the world through lust. (2 Pet. 1:2-4)

Do you see now that even though your sins are gone, this truth alone won't get you into Heaven? The truth is that God had to deal with your sins and your sin nature before you could even enter into Heaven. He did that for you through His only Son, Jesus Christ. Even though our sins are gone, the only way we can go to Heaven is to be born again of God's Spirit and receive His divine nature in our hearts. Because God has loved you enough to put away your sins, now you can be born again by believing in Jesus Christ.

Personal Study Notes

CHAPTER 7

THE
OPERATION
of GOD

Buried with him in baptism,
wherein also ye are risen with him through
the faith of the operation of God,
who hath raised him from the dead.

COL. 2:12

The Price Was Paid

Buried with Him in baptism, wherein also ye are *risen with Him through the faith of the operation of God*, who hath raised him from the dead. And you, being dead in your sins and the uncircumcision of your flesh, hath he quickened together with him, having forgiven you all trespasses; *Blotting out the handwriting of ordinances that was against us*, which was contrary to us, and took it out of the way, nailing it to his cross; And having spoiled principalities and powers, he made a shew of them openly, triumphing over them in it. (Col. 2:12-15)

God promised from the very beginning He was going to put a savior between Satan and mankind and that He would crush (the head of the serpent) Satan's authority and power of death over man. Jesus has done that. He came from Heaven to earth, walked with God, lived a perfect life and fulfilled the Law of God on our behalf. He was born of a virgin so Satan had no authority over Jesus through Adam's bloodline. Jesus said in John 14:30, "Hereafter I will not talk much with you: for the prince of this world cometh, and hath nothing in me." Jesus was born of a virgin so He was not a child of Adam and Satan had no place in Him. Death had no power over Him. He lived a perfect life on our behalf, to be our example and to become our substitute. Then He laid down His natural life (as our substitute) and defeated the powers of death for us so we might be given His divine nature and walk in His life.

At the cross God blotted out every commandment that we've ever broken and every judgment that was against us. That's where we were put to death in Christ. Jesus went to Hell and accomplished every punishment that was prepared for us. That's where we were punished in Christ. There in Hell, Jesus conquered Satan and destroyed his power of death over us. Then the Bible says, when we were declared righteous in His sight, God raised Jesus from the dead *for us*. The Battle was the Lord's but the victory is now ours.

Even as the Son of man came not to be ministered unto, but to minister, and to give his life a ransom for many. (Matt. 20:28)

> Who gave himself a ransom for all, to be testified in due time. (1 Tim. 2:6)

Jesus has historically given His life as a ransom for us. What Jesus has done for us is done and can't be undone. By Jesus laying down His life for us He became our true innocent sacrificial Lamb of God. Jesus allowed God to put our sins upon Him, our death upon Him, and our punishment in Hell upon Him. Three times in the Bible God spoke from Heaven, saying, ". . . this is my Son in whom I am well pleased." Just like the priest would examine the lamb to make sure it was without spot, even so God proved Jesus in His perfect earthly walk and was pleased with Him. Then God the Father put Jesus on the cross and crucified Him for us, just like Abraham put his son Isaac on the altar. Jesus was the only human ever born that was qualified to become the innocent sacrificial Lamb of God, which can take away our sins. Jesus died on the cross for us and then went to Hell for us, where God poured out His wrath toward us, upon Him. When God was satisfied with our punishment for sin, He raised Jesus from the dead *for us*. Jesus has become our eternal high priest who brings us back unto God. The price has been fully paid for us to have eternal life.

> Now it was not written for his sake alone, that it was imputed to him; But for us also, to whom it shall be imputed, if we believe on him that raised up Jesus our Lord from the dead; Who was delivered for our offences, and *was raised again for our justification.* (Rom. 4:23-25)

This scripture says, "When we were justified, He was raised from the dead." This scripture is another reason why I believe everything that happened from the cross to the throne was done for us. He was our substitute. He took everything that belonged to us so we can have everything that belongs to Him. The Bible is good news.

> Therefore doth my Father love me, because I lay down my life, that I might take it again. No man taketh it from me, but I lay it down of myself. I have power to lay it down, and I have power

to take it again. This commandment have I received of my Father. (John 10:17-18)

Greater love hath no man than this that a man lay down his life for his friends. (John 15:13)

The Operation of God

For the law having a shadow of good things to come, and not the very image of the things, can never with those sacrifices, which they offered year by year continually make the comers thereunto perfect. For then would they not have ceased to be offered because that the worshippers once purged should have had no more conscience of sins. But in those sacrifices there is a remembrance again made of sins every year. For it is not possible that the blood of bulls and of goats should take away sins. Wherefore when he cometh into the world, he saith, Sacrifice and offering thou wouldest not, but a body hast thou prepared me: In burnt offerings and sacrifices for sin thou hast had no pleasure. Then said I, Lo, I come (in the volume of the book it is written of me,) to do thy will, O God. Above when he said, Sacrifice and offering and burnt offerings and offering for sin thou wouldest not, neither hadst pleasure therein; which are offered by the law; Then said he, Lo, I come to do thy will, O God. He taketh away the first, that he may establish the second, By the which will we are sanctified through the offering of the body of Jesus Christ once for all. (Heb. 10:1-10)

Here in this passage of scripture we see the secret of eternity. I can see a time in eternity past, before creation, when the Son comes before the throne of God His Father, saying, "When, Father, when are we going to create that universe together that you promised me?" I can see the Heavenly Father responding to His only Son, saying, "Son, we'll do it after time begins. We'll create that universe together and the creature will fall away from our kingdom. They will make the same mistake Lucifer made, but I will create one of their bodies for you to put on, and send you down to visit with them, so you can tell them the truth and show them the life that is eternal. You will bring many of them back as my very own sons and our family will be enlarged just like we have been planning for ages now. Just be patient a little longer, Son."

Here we see Jesus as He is coming into this world, saying to God, "You weren't satisfied with constant sacrifices that point people to me, so you've prepared me a body and I come to earth to do your will, O God." He came to be our innocent sacrificial Lamb so God could lay our sins on Him, thereby reconciling us to Himself. That was the first thing God had to do before He could receive sinners like you and me into Heaven.

The Law of the Universe is, something must die so I might live. All throughout the Old Testament we see the fathers sacrificing innocent animals, demonstrating their faith in God's promise. We see the operation of God with Moses in the Tabernacle. God showed Israel the pictures of how He would do this through the tabernacle, the priesthood, and the sacrifices. The Twelve tribes of Israel surrounded the Tabernacle in the shape of a cross. There were three tribes in each direction: the north, the south, the east and the west. The Tabernacle was called the meeting place of God. The picture of the tabernacle shows us that we must all meet with God. We see the people coming to God in faith with their innocent sacrificial lambs, thereby procuring forgiveness of their sins. The head of the family would come to the priest with their lamb without spot; he would lay his hands upon the innocent animal and confess his sins. Then the priest killed the lamb and the blood was shed, the body was burned upon the altar, the sins of the family were forgiven, and they were temporarily reconciled unto God. After that, the High Priest would sprinkle the blood of the Lamb on the mercy seat of the Ark in the Tabernacle. Through this practice of sacrifices, God would forgive their sins. How would you like to do that on a regular basis in order to continue your fellowship with God?

And every priest standeth daily ministering and offering oftentimes the same sacrifices, which can never take away sins: But this man, after he had offered one sacrifice for sins forever, sat down on the right hand of God; From henceforth expecting till his enemies be made his footstool. For by one offering he hath perfected forever them that are sanctified. Whereof the Holy Ghost also is a witness to us: for after that he had said before, This is the covenant that I will make with them after those days, saith the Lord, I will put my laws into their hearts, and in their minds will I write them; And *their sins and iniquities will I remember no more*. Now where remission of these is, there is no more offering for sin. (Heb. 10:11-18)

Well, God wasn't satisfied with that practice either. God was doing it this way to point us to His Son, Jesus Christ, who would later come and die on the cross for us. The Bible says the Law served as a shadow of good things to come. The shadow is only the image of the real thing. This practice of ministry with the blood of bulls, lambs and goats, etc., couldn't make them perfect (give them the divine nature) because there was always a remembrance of sins. God needed a perfect human body without sin to accomplish our forgiveness of sins, so God prepared a body for Jesus in the womb of a virgin that didn't have Adam's sin nature in it. This made Jesus the perfect sacrifice by which God could take our sins from us and transfer them to Jesus while at the same time transferring Jesus' divine nature to us, making us righteous in His sight. In the next passage, we see this event perfectly described in the words of the prophet Isaiah as though it is taking place centuries before.

Who hath believed our report? and to whom is the arm of the LORD revealed? For he shall grow up before him as a tender plant, and as a root out of a dry ground: he hath no form nor comeliness; and when we shall see him, there is no beauty that we should desire him. He is despised and rejected of men; a man of sorrows, and acquainted with grief: and we hid as it were our faces from him; he was despised, and we esteemed him not. Surely he hath borne our griefs, and carried our sorrows: yet we did esteem him *stricken, smitten* of God, and *afflicted*. But he was wounded for our transgressions, he was bruised for our iniquities: the chastisement of our peace was upon him; and with his stripes we are healed. All we like sheep have gone astray; we have turned everyone to his own way; and the LORD hath laid on him the iniquity of us all. He was oppressed, and he was afflicted, yet he opened not his mouth: he is brought as a lamb to the slaughter, and as a sheep before her shearers is dumb, so he openeth not his mouth. He was taken from prison and from judgment: and who shall declare his generation? for he was cut off out of the land of the living: for the transgression of my people was he stricken. And he made his grave with the wicked, and with the rich in his death; because he had done no violence, neither was any deceit in his mouth. Yet it pleased the LORD to bruise him; he hath put him to grief: when thou shalt make his soul an offering for sin, he shall see his seed, he shall prolong his days, and the pleasure of the LORD shall prosper in his hand. He shall see of the travail of his soul, and shall be satisfied: by his knowledge shall my righteous servant justify many; for he shall bear their iniquities. Therefore, will I divide him a portion with the great, and he shall divide the spoil with the strong; because he hath poured out his soul unto death: and he was numbered with the transgressors; and he bare the sin of many, and made intercession for the transgressors. (Isa. 53:1-12)

Centuries before it happened, the prophet Isaiah prophesies these words like it has already happened, saying, "Who is going to believe this? He is going to grow up as a tender person, and we shall despise and reject Him. He has surely borne our sin nature and our sins, and like a lamb to the slaughter, He will be wounded, bruised and God will smite Him for us. Like a sheep being sheered, he won't even open His mouth and then He will be cut off as a sacrifice for many. But God will be pleased with Him and give Him an inheritance with many others. He will make many righteous and bring many sons unto glory." Long before it happened the prophet Isaiah basically said the secret of eternity is accomplished. God created a body for Jesus so He could come to earth, live the perfect life in our place, and then be sacrificed as our Lamb of God to remove sin from us. As Jesus was leaving Heaven and coming to Earth, He said, "Everything in the Bible is talking about me. Lo I come to do thy will O God." Just as He has always lived before God in eternity past, Jesus lived His whole life on earth in the presence of God and everywhere Jesus went people felt God's presence. That is eternal life and that is the life God meant for us to have, but Adam lost it for us in the Garden of Eden.

The Sign of Jonah

> But he answered and said unto them, An evil and adulterous gener-
> ation seeketh after a sign; and there shall no sign be given to it, but
> the sign of the prophet Jonas: For as Jonas was three days and three
> nights in the whale's belly; so shall the Son of man be three days and
> three *nights in the heart of the earth*. (Matt. 12:39-40)

Jesus could have told them the sign was the virgin birth. That was the sign
of the prophet Isaiah who said, "a virgin shall conceive." The virgin birth
was the fulfillment of the promise of Genesis 3:15, which says, "I will put
enmity between you Satan and the seed of the woman." Jesus could have
said the sign was the cross. That was where He was suspended between
Heaven and Earth for all creation to see with the sign above His head,
which read "King of the Jews." Jesus could have said the sign is the empty
tomb. That is truly the sign of history that death has been defeated. But
Jesus said the sign God is giving us is the sign of Jonah. Why did Jesus consider Jonah to be the most important sign for us to see? Jesus gave us the
answer, saying, "Just as Jonah was in the belly of the whale for three days
and nights, so must the Son of Man spend three days and nights in the
heart of the earth in the place called Hell." That is where He would suffer
things beyond our imaginations. Just like the scapegoat bore away the sins
of the nation as it went into the uninhabitable places of the desert, even so
Jesus bore away our sins as He descended into Hell *for us*. The Bible says the
wages of sin is death, but if the wages of sin is death, what is the penalty
of sin? It is Hell.

> Then Jonah prayed to the LORD his God from the fish's belly. And
> he said: "I cried out to the LORD because of my affliction, And He
> answered me. *"Out of the belly of Sheol I cried*, And You heard my voice.
> For You cast me into the deep, Into the heart of the seas, And the
> floods surrounded me; All Your billows and Your waves passed over
> me. Then I said, *'I have been cast out of Your sight*; Yet I will look again
> toward Your holy temple.' The waters surrounded me, even to my
> soul; The deep closed around me; Weeds were wrapped around my
> head. *I went down* to the moorings of the mountains; *The earth with its*

bars closed behind me forever; Yet *You have brought up my life from the pit,* O LORD, my God. "When my soul fainted within me, I remembered the LORD; And my prayer went up to You, Into Your holy temple. "Those who regard worthless idols Forsake their own Mercy. But I will sacrifice to You With the voice of thanksgiving; I will pay what I have vowed. Salvation is of the LORD." So the LORD spoke to the fish, and it vomited Jonah onto dry land. (John 2:1-10)

Jesus said just as Jonah spent three days and nights in the belly of the whale, even so He must spend three days and nights in the heart of the earth or, in this scripture, "the belly of Hell." Jesus died on the cross for us and then He went to Hell for three days and nights. Just like Jesus lived and died as our substitute, I believe He went to Hell for us as our substitute. Jesus said the sign for us was the sign of Jonah. To us the cross was the sign. It was definitely God's billboard. The sign above Jesus' head was written in three languages that He was the King of the Jews. But Jesus said the sign for the human race was His trip to Hell. He said, "just like Jonah was in the belly of the whale for three days and nights, even so must He spend three days and nights in Hell." There is no greater predicament in eternity than the perfect Son of God, the king of Heaven, spending three days and nights in Hell. Do you think He did that for Himself? There is no point. The only reason He went to Hell was for me and for you.

Of whom we have many things to say, and hard to be uttered, seeing ye are dull of hearing. (Heb. 5:11 NKJV)

This subject about Jesus going to Hell is one of those things that are hard to utter because I wasn't there and I can only go by the scriptures and the enlightenment of the Spirit of God. I believe Jesus was punished in Hell for us and I explain in greater detail what happened in Hell in our volume 2 of the Secrets of the Bible series, which is entitled *Death and Life, Secret of the Bible.* Many believers have a problem thinking about Jesus going to Hell and would believe that what Jesus did on the cross was enough to open the doors of Heaven for us. I believe the cross is only the beginning of what Jesus did for us. I believe the Old Testament types bear witness to these things. There were a number of things Jesus did and accomplished in Hell during those three days and nights as part of the operation of God.

Then, when the demands of God's standard of divine justice was satisfied, God raised Jesus from the dead for us, to give us the sign that His life and death is accepted in our place. The virgin birth, the empty tomb and the resurrection of Christ are all signs to us that Satan's powers of death over us have been abolished and we are free to come back into fellowship with God again. That way we can come into agreement with God by faith, accept His life, death, burial, and resurrection for us, as our own, and through faith receive His divine nature, making us fit for Heaven. As we believe in Christ and His substitutionary work for us, God grafts us into Christ, we become alive unto God and begin to partake of His divine nature. That's the way God sees us right now. As far as God is concerned, when Jesus was on the cross, we were on the cross. God did what only God can do. He put everything we are in the first creation, into Christ and smote it *for us*, and by resurrection, He transported us into the new creation in Christ.

> For he hath made him to be sin for us, who knew no sin; that we might be made the righteousness of God in him. (2 Cor. 5:21)

The cross was where the operation of God began. Just as God put all human beings into the first Adam, He put us into the last Adam, who is Christ, and transferred our sinful human nature we inherited from Adam to Jesus. Jesus provided God with a physical body in which God could put every human just like Adam, and perform His operation upon the cross. God didn't just transfer our sins to Jesus like He did in the Old Testament when the sins of the human were transferred to sacrificial lambs, but the Bible says Jesus was *made to be sin for us* as our substitute. Then just as the carcasses were burned in the fire, Jesus went to Hell and suffered in our place.

The Bible says He was raised for our justification. That means when we were declared righteous in God's sight, God raised Jesus from the dead, and when He was raised, we were raised from the dead together with Him. As far as God is concerned it is finished. Now whether we receive God's gift of eternal life or not, whether we believe what the Bible says or not, that is our choice, our responsibility, and our issue. God has essentially brought us back to the same position where Adam was in the Garden of Eden.

> And *you He made alive, who were dead* in trespasses and sins, in which you once walked according to the course of this world, according to the prince of the power of the air, the spirit who now works in the sons of disobedience, among whom also we all once conducted ourselves in the lusts of our flesh, fulfilling the desires of the flesh and of the mind, and were by nature children of wrath, just as the others. But God, who is rich in mercy, because of His great love with which He loved us, even when we were dead in trespasses, made us alive together with Christ (by grace you have been saved), and raised us up together, and made us sit together in the heavenly places in Christ Jesus, that in the ages to come He might show the exceeding riches of His grace in His kindness toward us in Christ Jesus. For *by grace* you have been saved *through faith*, and that not of yourselves; *it is the gift of God*, not of works, lest anyone should boast. For we are His workmanship, created in Christ Jesus for good works, which God prepared beforehand that we should walk in them. (Eph. 2:1-10 NKJV)

What happened from the cross to the throne, the apostle Paul calls the *operation of God*. When Jesus said, "It is finished," I believe He was talking about the operation of God. God has done it all. Through Jesus, God has abolished death *for us* and through the preaching of the gospel God brings life and immortality to light. Notice in these scriptures it describes everything God did in past tense. Only God can do surgery upon our human spirits. God is a supernatural God and He has performed supernatural surgery upon the human race. He did that on the cross.

The Sign of Noah

> Heaven and earth will pass away, but My words will by no means pass away. "But of that day and hour no one knows, not even the angels of heaven, but My Father only. But *as the days of Noah* were, so also will the coming of the Son of Man be. For as in the days

before the flood, they were eating and drinking, marrying and giving in marriage, until the day that Noah entered the ark, and did not know until the flood came and took them all away, so also will the coming of the Son of Man be. (Matt. 24:35-39)

Remember, in everything God does, He teaches something. Jesus gives us another "just as it was in the days of" with Noah to ponder about. Noah and his family built an ark in obedience to God. When the time of the flood came, they were carried by that ark into the new world while the old world was being destroyed. Jesus said multitudes of people would be lost just like they were lost in the days of Noah. People were caught up in the affairs of life and they didn't know any change was taking place until the flood destroyed them and it was too late. But Noah walked with God and heard God's voice. Noah followed God's instructions and prepared his family and they were saved. By condemning the way of the world in his heart he became a righteous believer in God's sight. God's way of instructing Noah to be ready for what was surely coming is the way God instructs us in the Bible to get ready for eternity. God is also teaching us through Noah about the operation of God that was accomplished for you in Jesus Christ. Just like God made provision for Noah to be saved from things to come through the ark, He has also provided for us an ark through Jesus Christ. Will you also walk with God, hear God's voice and follow God's instructions?

By faith Noah, being warned of God of things not seen as yet, *moved with fear*, prepared an ark to the saving of his house; by the which *he condemned the world*, and *became heir* of the righteousness which is by faith. (Heb. 11:7)

God separated Noah from everything that belonged to the world and preserved him for the world to come. Even so in Christ, God separated us from our spiritually dead nature in Adam, from our bondage to the world system and from the world's judgment and destruction. Just as God shut the door of the ark for Noah, even so God put us into Christ upon the cross and Jesus became our ark. I believe everything we were in the first creation in Adam was destroyed when Jesus died. Just like the ark passed through the waves that destroyed the first creation, into the new world that was clean before God, I believe Jesus carried us through the waves of God's wrath in Hell and preserved us for eternity. Can you see the goodness of God that no religion can provide? Do you feel the need to move with fear to the saving of your soul?

> Buried with him in baptism, wherein also ye are risen with him through the faith of the operation of God, who hath raised him from the dead. (Col. 2:12)

> Therefore we are buried with him by baptism into death: that like as Christ was raised up from the dead by the glory of the Father, even so we also should walk in newness of life. (Rom. 6:4)

God isn't just showing us what happened to Jesus in the Bible. God is showing us what He has done to us through Jesus in the Bible. God's operation was supernatural surgery upon the spirits of men. What God did to Jesus He was doing unto us and the two signs of Jonah and Noah are our examples. God put us in Christ upon the cross, He took us through Hell in Christ and He brought us through to the other side in Christ. Just like Noah came out of the ark to walk with God in a brand-new world, even so God makes all things new as we believe in the Operation of God. The power of God is activated inside our spirits by faith the moment we believe in the Operation of God. Do you see the need to be like Noah and become an heir of the righteousness, which is by faith?

> Now it was not written for his sake alone, that it was imputed to him; But for us also, to whom it shall be imputed, if we believe on him that raised up Jesus our Lord from the dead; Who was delivered for our offences, and was *raised again for our justification*. (Rom. 4:23-25)

The Bible says, when we were justified (declared righteous in God's sight), Jesus was raised for us. That means when God was finished punishing you and me in Christ, He raised Jesus from the dead. Just as our sins were transferred to Jesus, His divine nature was transferred to us, making us clean to walk with God in His presence. Then the Bible says in Ephesians chapter two, when God raised Jesus from the dead He raised you and me from the dead and declared us righteous in His sight. That is the way God sees us right now. He sees our sins are gone, and we now stand before Him wearing the spiritual garments of the righteousness of Jesus Christ, if we believe in the operation of God.

> Wherefore he saith, When he ascended up on high, he led captivity captive, and gave gifts unto men. Now that he ascended, what is it but that he also descended first into the lower parts of the earth? He that descended is the same also that ascended up far above all heavens, that he might fill all things. (Eph. 4:8-10)

To save us, Jesus had to die so He could conquer death for us. Our blood had the serpent's poison of sin in it. His blood has the antidote of the life of God in it. The Bible says in Romans 7:1-5 and 2 Corinthians 11:2 that Jesus died to help us die to our first husband (Satan through the curse of the law), so we could be released from our bondage to death being dead to the law, and be married to another (Christ). God swore an oath to us and His oath is His covenant to us. The Bible uses the typical marriage covenant as an example to prove the issue. Just like the marriage covenant is in force until death, even so God's oath to us is an eternal covenant. It says, when the husband dies the woman is loosed from the law of the oath she has made to her husband and is free to remarry. God is showing us here in the natural what took place in the spiritual through the operation of God. When we believe in the operation of God and receive God's eternal provision for us through the Son of God, we literally pass from death to life. Roman 7:1-6 says, "We die to our first spiritual husband who brought us into bondage to death, and we are made alive unto our new spiritual husband which is Jesus Christ, our redeemer, that is alive forevermore." This knowledge should strengthen your faith.

- ✔ We were born in sin
- ✔ We are in bondage to death
- ✔ We are destined for Hell

Without the power of God, we are doomed forever. Through the operation of God, the grace of God hunted us down and provided the solution, the cure and the gift of love. So what was the cure? It is the Tree of Life. The cross was a dead tree with the eternal Son of God on it. The cross became the Tree of Life for us. The cross of Jesus is the portal into Heaven. Adam failed to eat of the Tree of Life. So God sent His Son, Jesus, from Heaven to earth, to become the Tree of Life for us. By eating of the Tree of Knowledge Adam took in the death program (knowledge of the universe without God), which has been transferred to all of us who are Adam's progeny. Even so Jesus was lifted up upon the cross so that all who eat of that tree will live forever. God provided Jesus upon the cursed tree of the cross as the way to get the death out and the life in. The horizontal bar of the cross represents all of sinful humanity from the east to the west. The vertical bar of the cross represents all the love of God from Heaven to Earth. The gift upon the cross was Jesus, the Son of God. When Jesus stretched out His arms wide upon the cross He was saying, "I love you this much and I want you in Heaven with me." When we believe in Jesus, we eat of the Tree of Life and become new creatures in Him. When grace calls and faith answers, the love of God is born.

> But we speak *the wisdom of God in a mystery*, even the *hidden wisdom*, which God ordained before the world unto our glory: Which none of the princes of this world knew: for had they known it, they would not have crucified the Lord of glory. But as it is written, Eye hath not seen, nor ear heard, neither have entered into the heart of man, the things which God hath prepared for them that love him. But God hath revealed them unto us by his Spirit: for the Spirit searcheth all things, yea, the deep things of God. (1 Cor. 2:7-10)

The Bible says the angels (principalities and powers) are beholding the manifold wisdom and love of God through the operation of God, by the Church. The angels saw the rebellion of the angel Lucifer in Heaven and watched his nature change as he became Satan. The angels saw God create the worlds and the human race. The angels watched Satan engineer man's rebellion against God and bring the universe under the curse of death. Then the angels saw our nature change as the Father and the Son wrought redemption to all creation through the operation of God. The angels know who the true believers are. It's beyond our imagination how God could re-create multitudes of people from the first creation in Adam into new creations in the last Adam, Jesus Christ. The Bible says it's the hidden wisdom that God purposed before creation to accomplish. The Bible says, "Had the angelic powers (Satan and his hosts) of this world known, they would not have crucified the Lord of Glory."

> For it pleased the Father that in him should all fullness dwell. (Col. 1:19)

No power of any creature in Heaven or Earth can match the creative power of God the Father and His Son, by His Spirit. Unlike Adam's disobedience, now through Jesus' obedience to God, the King of Heaven has become the King of kings in Heaven and earth and Jesus alone can be trusted to do what is good for man. Just as our first birth was the gift of God, even so the new birth is the gift of God through Jesus Christ. That is the message for this mess-Age. How does this wonderful gift get activated? It happens the moment we believe the truth and receive Jesus as Lord. But not everyone will believe in Jesus and not everyone will receive the gift of God. But God has ordained that in His Son should all creation dwell.

> Wherein in time past ye walked according to the course of this world, according to the prince of the power of the air, the spirit that now worketh in the children of disobedience. (Eph. 2:2)

Even though we are forgiven of all sin, we can't go to be with God the way we were born. Our nature is wrong. As we are, we live by a spirit of disobedience, which feeds upon knowledge without God, and in that spiritual state we are incompatible with God, unfit for Heaven and headed for Hell. The Bible says we are born with the spirit of disobedience. Humans never have to teach a child how to do wrong; he does wrong by nature, and we have to teach him what is right. The Bible says, just like an Ethiopian can't change the color of his skin or the leopard his spots, neither can we change the nature of our hard hearts. That's why being moral and doing good deeds can't save us. But God in His love can change us, and through the new birth He does change us if we allow Him to. Jesus said, "Ye must be born again." Through faith in the operation of God, He gives us a new Spirit, and we receive the divine nature of Christ. God puts a new spirit in us and gives us a new heart. The reason we get born again is to receive God's divine nature.

> And I will give them one heart, and I will put a new spirit within you; and I will take the stony heart out of their flesh, and will give them an heart of flesh: That they may walk in my statutes, and keep mine ordinances, and do them: and they shall be my people, and I will be their God. (Ezek. 11:19-20)

God takes out the stony heart, which is hard as a rock in the self program, and gives us a new heart that can love God and believe in the goodness of God. This is something only God can do. The new birth makes us compatible with God, fit for Heaven and a citizen of God's family. And while we're here, because we have His divine nature, we can walk with Him in the same way Jesus walked with the heavenly Father. That is what eternal life is, a Father and Son walk—forever.

> Whereby are given unto us exceeding great and precious promises: that by these ye might be partakers of the divine nature, *having escaped* the corruption that is in the world through lust. (2 Pet. 1:4)

Not as it was with Adam, even so it is with Christ. Just as everything Adam did affected us, even so everything Jesus did affects you and me if Christ is in us. As far as God is concerned, when we believe in the operation of God, we have escaped from the corrupt heart with the death program and His perfect life is now our life. His obedience is our obedience. His death, burial, and resurrection belong to us because the Spirit of Christ who went through all those things now lives in us. God sees no difference between Him and us, if we believe. If Christ is in us now, then we are growing up into Him in all things, the Bible says. We are no longer children of the devil, but children of the one true God. As far as God is concerned, even though you were once dead to God, now you are dead (to sin) and alive unto God through Christ in you. Have you received this provision of life that Christ died to give you?

> If ye then be risen with Christ, seek those things, which are above, where Christ sitteth on the right hand of God. Set your affection on things above, not on things on the earth For ye are dead, and *your life is hid with Christ in God*. When Christ, who is our life, shall appear, then shall ye also appear with Him in glory. (Col. 3:1-4)

The operation of God was the climax of the Bible. God isn't just forgiving our sins and taking us to Heaven. God is having a family. God is re-creating us into new creatures in Christ, fit to live in Heaven. God calls it eternal life. Jesus called it the New Birth. The Bible calls it the Divine Nature. God did the surgery in His only Son upon His operating table of the cross. Can you see the practicality of the operation of God? Can you enter into the experience of the operation of God? It took God thousands of years to perform the surgery, but it only takes a few seconds for God's surgery upon your spirit to be activated in your heart. It happens when you hear the truth, believe the truth, and confess Jesus as your Lord and Savior. That's when you become the righteousness of God in Christ.

> For I am not ashamed of the gospel of Christ: for *it is the power of God* unto salvation to everyone that believeth; to the Jew first, and also to the Greek. For *therein is the righteousness of God revealed* from faith to faith: as it is written, the just shall live by faith. (Rom. 1:16-17)

The Serpent in the Wilderness

> And as Moses lifted up the serpent in the wilderness, even so must the Son of man be lifted up: That whosoever believeth in him should not perish, but have eternal life. For God so loved the world, that he gave his only begotten Son, that whosoever believeth in him should not perish, but have everlasting life. (John 3:15-16)

Again, remember in everything God does, He teaches something. In this passage of scripture Jesus is talking with Nicodemus and He brings up how we believe ourselves into Christ by faith. He points us to the cross.

The first part of faith is seeing and believing how God put us in Christ. That is the natural part. The last part of faith is seeing and believing how God forms Christ in us. We can't see Christ in us now without seeing us in Christ on the cross. And we can't be healed of the poison of sin without seeing Christ in us.

Here's how the new birth works. Jesus said, "The earthly thing in the Old Testament that reveals the heavenly thing in the New Testament is the serpent in the wilderness." We have this condition inside us that they had in the wilderness. We are all the same spiritually, no matter what our culture, our color, or our status is. We are never truly satisfied with our earthly nature because something inside us knows we were created for eternity. We were created to be spiritual, but we can only see we are natural and the human spirit isn't satisfied with that. Worshipping idols, saying prayers, obeying religion etc., puts us to work but doesn't make us spiritual. Reincarnation and evolution have no scientific proof but the resurrection of Jesus is history and reality.

Nicodemus came to Jesus because something was bothering him. He knew Jesus was a man of God in truth yet he knew they were the people of God and as a spiritual leader He represented the law of God. So why is there friction with the religious leaders about Jesus all the time? Religion and truth can never be friends. As Nicodemus began talking with Him, Jesus didn't even respond to what Nicodemus was saying but went right to the heart of the matter, which is the most important thing the human needs to know about. The very first thing Jesus said to Nicodemus was, "You must be born again." Then Jesus said how He was going to make the new birth possible by the cross. Jesus said, "Just like the serpent was lifted up in the wilderness, even so must the Son of man be lifted up that whosoever believes in him might have eternal life." God wants us to have eternal life.

All God asks you to do is believe what He is telling you in the Bible He has done for you and you will be saved. The whole Bible is about God giving us eternal life. What was Jesus trying to get across to Nicodemus by reminding him of the serpent upon the pole? The people in the wilderness who were bitten by serpents are a picture of us. In Adam the serpent bit us all. We are all dying from the poison of sin. This is another time in the Old Testament where God points us to the operation of God and the new birth, which the New Testament reveals Jesus has accomplished for us. Jesus said,

"As the serpent was lifted in the wilderness, even so must the Son of man be lifted up so we can believe and be healed and saved."

In the 21st chapter of the book of Numbers, the Bible gives us an account of the brass serpent. In the wilderness the people of Israel were murmuring against God and Moses. The people weren't satisfied with God's heavenly provision in the desert. As they murmured against God, they were being bitten by serpents and dying. It's just like God to show us that when we murmur against God because we aren't satisfied with Him, we are really being bitten by devils and we are dying. They started crying out to God for a solution to keep them from dying. So Moses went to God about it and God told Moses to make a fiery brass serpent, put it on a pole and lift it up for all to see. Everyone who looks at the serpent will live and those who won't look at the serpent will die. This doesn't make sense to the natural man, but to the spiritual man it makes perfect sense. So Moses obeyed God and a statue of the fiery brass serpent was made and lifted up for all to see in the wilderness. The people who looked at the serpent in faith lived. Those who failed to look at the serpent in faith died. It didn't make natural sense for someone to look at a brass serpent on a pole and be healed of the poisons of the snakes that were biting them. Such is the case with the natural man. In the natural man, every time we sin we are being bitten by the devil, and we are dying spiritually. In Adam it is our nature to sin. The natural man sees when the serpent bites him and the poison spreads throughout his body, and he believes he is going to die. Those who looked at the brass serpent that was lifted up on the pole lived. Those who refused to look at the brass serpent died.

In the Bible, brass represents judgment. To me the fiery brass represents the judgment of Hell. Brass looks similar to purified gold but it is darker and less glorious. On the Day of Judgment when our hearts are tried before God, we will either be as pure as gold or corrupt like brass in God's sight. Gold is greater in glory than brass. God purifies our hearts like gold. He sees our faith as pure gold. The brass serpent represents Satan, the one by which we are satisfied living life without God. The pole lifted up represents the cross where Jesus would be lifted up for the world to see and where Satan (the serpent) and sin would be judged. God was showing them the cross that was yet to come. The cross is where God would judge Satan and his children. As God performed His operation, He put the whole human race into the body of Jesus Christ (just like Adam) and then, in Christ, we descended into Hell (just like Jonah). When Jesus rose again, our sins were gone and we were declared righteous (just like Noah) before God. That's the way God sees us now.

> That it might be fulfilled which was spoken by Esaias the prophet, saying, Himself took our infirmities, and bare our sicknesses. (Matt. 8:17)

Here we see another aspect of God's complete provision for us. God left nothing out. God not only destroyed the powers of death for us but He also healed us of our diseases. Jesus healed everyone that came to Him in faith. Jesus never refused to heal anyone. In His death, He took our diseases with Him. He said to Nicodemus it would happen the same way it happened with the serpent upon the pole. The spiritual man believes God no matter what the natural man is telling him. In the wilderness, when they looked at the serpent on the pole in faith, the snake poisons in their bodies had no effect. Jesus said in the same way, He had to die on the cross that all men who look at the cross and believe in Him might be healed and be saved.

> And he went a little further, and fell on his face, and prayed, saying, O my Father, if it be possible, let this cup pass from me: nevertheless not as I will, but as thou wilt. (Matt. 26:39)

Have you ever thought, why did Jesus have to die on the cross? Jesus laid down His life so God could put Him on the cross. When Jesus was on the cross, He and God were doing something only they could do. Just like God put every human being ever born into Adam, even so God put every human being born of Adam into Christ upon the cross. I believe the process of God putting us into Christ began when He was praying in the Garden of Gethsemane. Jesus began to sweat great drops of blood and He said, "If it be thy will, Father take this cup from me." This was where Jesus received strength from God as He aligned His will with God's will.

> Who his own self bare our sins in his own body on the tree that we, being dead to sins, should live unto righteousness: by whose stripes ye were healed. (1 Pet. 2:24)

Then after His mock trial, the Bible says, through the lashes of the whip, ". . . himself bore our sins, our infirmities, and sicknesses, and by His stripes we were healed." I believe this is where God transferred all our sicknesses and diseases to Him and we were healed. Science has determined that all human sicknesses fall into thirty-nine strains. Jesus took thirty-nine stripes and His flesh was ripped to shreds by the Roman whip (cat-o'-nine-tails) for us. With every lash of the whip God was transferring our diseases into His body. Jesus was becoming our substitute. Jesus said, "Just like the serpent on the pole, so it had to be with the Son of God upon the cross." So why then did they have to look at the serpent in order to live? It is because we have to look at the cross in order to live. Just like they had to look at the serpent on the pole in order to live, God is saying to us we have to look at the cross in order to live. If we won't look at the cross, we will die. What happens when we look at the cross? When we look up at the cross, whom do we see? By the eye of faith, we see ourselves in Christ and when we see that, we see everything that belongs to us from this world being transferred to Him. We also see everything that belongs to Him being transferred to us.

> *I am crucified with Christ*: nevertheless I live; yet not I, but *Christ liveth in me*: and the life which I now live in the flesh I live by the faith of the Son of God, who loved me, and gave himself for me. (Gal. 2:20)

If we look at the cross in faith, we see the judgment that should've fallen upon us being taken by our substitute. We also see ourselves being crucified in Christ, dying to sin. Now if we see ourselves dying up there on the cross in Christ, then who is living in us right now? It is Christ who is living in us now and we are healed of the poisons of sin, which came from the serpent's (Satan) bite. When I look at the cross and see myself in Christ Jesus, it changes me. I see it is no longer me who is living now, but Christ is living in me now. Just like Jesus became my substitute in death upon the cross, even so He is now my substitute in life. If you can see yourself in the first Adam in the Garden of Eden, then you can see yourself in the last Adam upon the cross. That is where we receive God's medicine that heals us for eternity. As in the natural, so it is in the spiritual. If you don't take God's medicine, it won't benefit you. But that's not all. There's more. God's medicine is also vitamins.

Then Jesus said unto them, Verily, verily, I say unto you, except ye eat the flesh of the Son of man, and drink his blood, *ye have no life in you.* Whoso eateth my flesh, and drinketh my blood, hath eternal life; and I will raise him up at the last day. For my flesh is meat indeed, and my blood is drink indeed. He that eateth my flesh, and drinketh my blood, dwelleth in me, and I in him. (John 6:53-56)

The Jews thought Jesus was crazy saying that. Imagine someone saying to you, "Unless you eat my flesh and drink my blood you have no life in you." God isn't just giving us medicine (His blood) to get the death out. God is also giving us vitamins (His flesh) to get the life in. Jesus is saying that to us. Eating His flesh is the principle of living by His ways that He lived by in the flesh. Drinking His blood is the principle that we trust in Jesus as our Lamb to cleanse us from sin and clothe us in His righteousness so we can walk in the light of fellowship with God and truly live.

But *we speak the wisdom of God in a mystery, even the hidden wisdom,* which God ordained before the world unto our glory: Which none of the princes of this world knew: for had they known it, they would not have crucified the Lord of glory. But as it is written, Eye hath not seen, nor ear heard, neither have entered into the heart of man, the things which God hath prepared for them that love him. But *God hath revealed them unto us* by his Spirit: for the Spirit searcheth all things, yea, the deep things of God. (1 Cor. 2:7-10)

Everything Satan did to the human race in Adam is now temporary. Everything that God did to the human race in Christ is now permanent and eternal. The operation of God was a complete success. Jesus has defeated death for us. Jesus now has all authority in Heaven and earth. We can now walk in the presence of God again through Christ in us. We enter into God's heavenly provision by faith. The Bible says we walk by faith, not by sight. For believers, eternity has begun. Just like when a new president is elected and he is the president elect for a time until his transition is complete and he becomes the actual president, even so planet Earth is going through the president-elect period. Yes, it has been over two thousand years since Jesus died on the cross, rose from the dead and left us with an empty tomb, but time is only a few minutes in eternity. Soon and very soon Jesus will return to set up His kingdom that will have no end. When He returns the whole creation will be brought back into submission to the heavenly Father for all eternity.

Personal Study Notes

CHAPTER 8

YOU *Must* BE BORN AGAIN

Marvel not that I said unto thee,
Ye must be born again.

JOHN 3:7

The New Birth

> Now this I say, brethren, that flesh and blood cannot inherit the kingdom of God; neither doth corruption inherit incorruption. (1 Cor. 15:50)

The Bible teaches spiritual birth works the same way as natural birth. Just as we were born by natural parents, even so we must be born again into God's Kingdom by His Spirit. God wants everyone to join Him in Heaven. But you must be born again of His divine nature. Just like you were born of man, you also must be born again of God. We can't go to Heaven as a natural man. The natural man is incompatible with God and unfit for Heaven.

> Being born again, not of corruptible seed, but of incorruptible, by the word of God, which liveth and abideth forever. (1 Pet. 1:23)

The new birth is the rebirth of the human spirit. The new birth is the only way for the human to become a spiritual man, united with the Spirit of Christ. You must invite Christ into your heart before the miracle of the new birth can take place. Through the power of the measure of faith, and His divine nature, our nature changes and we become citizens of Heaven. Just like Adam's nature changed when he disobeyed God in the Garden of Eden, even so our spiritual nature changes when we obey God by receiving His Son, Jesus Christ.

You Must Be Born of God

> There was a man of the Pharisees, named Nicodemus, a ruler of the Jews: The same came to Jesus by night, and said unto him, Rabbi, we know that thou art a teacher come from God: for no man can do these miracles that thou doest, except God be with him. Jesus answered and said unto him, Verily, verily, I say unto thee, Except a man be born again, *he cannot see the kingdom* of God. Nicodemus saith unto him, How can a man be born when he is old? Can he enter the

second time into his mother's womb, and be born? Jesus answered, Verily, verily, I say unto thee, Except a man be born of water and of the Spirit, *he cannot enter into the kingdom* of God. That which is born of the flesh is flesh; and that which is born of the Spirit is spirit. Marvel not that I said unto thee, *Ye must be born again*. The wind bloweth where it listeth, and thou hearest the sound thereof, but canst not tell whence it cometh, and whither it goeth: so is every one that is born of the Spirit. Nicodemus answered and said unto him, *How can these things be*? Jesus answered and said unto him, Art thou a master of Israel, and knowest not these things? Verily, verily, I say unto thee, We speak that we do know, and testify that we have seen; and ye receive not our witness. *If I have told you earthly things, and ye believe not, how shall ye believe, if I tell you of heavenly things*? And no man hath ascended up to heaven, but he that came down from heaven, even the Son of man, which is in heaven. And as Moses lifted up the serpent in the wilderness, even so must the Son of man be lifted up: That whosoever believeth in him should not perish, but have eternal life. For *God so loved* the world, that he gave his only begotten Son, that whosoever believeth in him should not perish, but have everlasting life. (John 3:1-16)

This may be a lot of scripture for you to read all at once but there is a conversation going on in which Jesus explains the issue between Heaven and Earth, between God and man. Jesus said, "We must be born again." There are very few times Jesus says in the Bible you *must* do something. This is one of those times. For this purpose, Jesus suffered beyond belief, died on the cross and rose again, just so you can be born again and become citizens of Heaven.

Let's examine the conversation Jesus had with Nicodemus because this conversation is the heart of the Bible. Nicodemus was a Pharisee. The Pharisees were the spiritual leaders of Israel. In the end they persecuted Jesus and demanded that Jesus be crucified because He taught that He was the Son of God. Their law said if a man claims to be Messiah and His claims are false he should be killed. But if the claims of the man are true then he should sit upon the throne of his father David as the king forever. Jesus claimed to be the Son of God and His genealogies lined up. Jesus knew what He was doing. They had two choices of how to respond. You know how they responded.

Some of the Pharisees believed in Jesus. Look at what Nicodemus said to Jesus. He said, "*We know* you are a teacher come from God because no man can do these miracles you are doing except God be with him." That's pretty sound minded. Remember the scripture "He shall be called Emmanuel, which means God is *with us*"? The Pharisees knew God was with Jesus. They could clearly see God was with Jesus. Nicodemus just said that. Let's continue in the conversation. Jesus didn't even respond to what Nicodemus said. Jesus just went to the heart of the truth. He said, "Except a man be born again he cannot see the Kingdom of God."

Nicodemus responded by saying, "How can a man be born again? Shall he enter into his mother's womb a second time and be born?" Nicodemus knew Jesus was talking about a new birth. Jesus went right back to the heart of the matter, again saying, "Except a man be born of water and Spirit, he cannot enter the Kingdom of God." Notice Jesus said, "I have spoken to you of earthly things and you do not believe; how then will you believe if I speak of heavenly things?" Jesus said the New Birth is a heavenly thing. Jesus uses the natural to explain the spiritual. Animals can't be born again as humans, but humans can be born again as spirit beings and become the children of God.

Here we see there are two phases of operation in the new birth. First, the eyes of the human must be opened. Jesus said if we aren't born again we *cannot see* the Kingdom of God. This happens as revelation comes through the words of God. Then Jesus said if we aren't born again we *cannot enter* the Kingdom of God. The Spirit of God must quicken the human spirit to make us alive unto God.

If you take a minute to ponder this thought, I think you will see it. God wants you to see this. If you can't see it, you won't get it. Remember, in everything God does, He teaches something. The natural is the clue of the spiritual. Just as it is in the natural so it is in the spiritual even though it is impossible. The natural comes first before the spiritual just like a seed comes before the tree. The spiritual comes after the natural just like the tree comes out of the seed. Without the seed there is no tree and without the tree there is no fruit. The fruit is where the life is. The fruit contains a multitude of seeds. In many passages of scripture humans are called trees, some good trees and some bad trees. We must go from being bad trees to being good trees. Jesus said you must be born again. Just as we are born in the natural, we must be born again into God's family. He said that which is born of the flesh is flesh and that which is born of the Spirit is our spirit.

> Jesus answered, Verily, verily, I say unto thee, except a man be born of water and of the Spirit, he cannot enter into the kingdom of God. That which is born of the flesh is flesh; and that which is born of the Spirit is spirit. Marvel not that I said unto thee, Ye must be born again. The wind bloweth where it listeth, and thou hearest the sound thereof, but canst not tell whence it cometh, and whither it goeth: so is every one that is born of the Spirit. (John 3:5-8)

Jesus said we must be born again or we *cannot see* the Kingdom of God and then He said we must be born again or we *cannot enter* the Kingdom of God. These are the two phases of faith. We must see the truth and then we must believe the truth so we can enter into the truth.

Think about it! Jesus always said what He meant and He always meant what He said. Most of the time Jesus spoke in parables, but not to Nicodemus. Remember the principle of the *Secret Language*: in everything God does, He teaches something. God even shows us from the first birth we must be born again. We can all understand we must be born of the Spirit just as we can see a baby must be born of the flesh to enter into planet Earth. Jesus said we shouldn't marvel about this. You must be born again. It is that simple. Then Jesus said, "If I tell you of earthly things and you can't believe me, how will you believe me when I tell you of heavenly things?" Jesus used earthly things to give us mental pictures of heavenly things. He said if you can't understand earthly things then you won't be able to understand spiritual things.

> For whatsoever is born of God overcometh the world: and this is the victory that overcometh the world, even our faith. (1 John 5:4)

The Bible says when we are born again, it is a victory and the victory is we are overcoming everything the world has trained us to think and to be in this world. When we come into agreement with God and are born again, we are more than conquerors, the Bible says. The world doesn't understand these things. The world thinks believers in Christ are strange. Just like you overcame the weaknesses of your mother's womb to be born of the flesh, so also you must overcome the peer pressures of the world to come to God. Even so you must overcome the tendencies of the flesh to live by the ways of death, in order to live and walk, as a child of God should.

> So also is the resurrection of the dead. It is sown in corruption; it is raised in incorruption: It is sown in dishonor; it is raised in glory: it is sown in weakness; it is raised in power: It is sown a natural body; it is raised a spiritual body. There is a natural body, and there is a spiritual body. And so it is written, The first man Adam was made a living soul; the last Adam was made a quickening spirit. Howbeit that was not first which is spiritual, but that which is natural; and afterward that which is spiritual. The first man is of the earth, earthy: the second man is the Lord from heaven. As is the earthy, such are they also that are earthy: and as is the heavenly, such are they also that are heavenly. And as we have borne the image of the earthy, we shall also bear the image of the heavenly. Now this I say, brethren, that flesh and blood cannot inherit the kingdom of God; neither doth corruption inherit incorruption. (1 Cor. 15:42-50)

Not as it is in the natural, so also it is in the spiritual. The natural is the image of the spiritual. We cannot go to Heaven as we are. Our spiritual nature is earthy. Jesus said, "That which is born of the flesh is flesh." The first man is of the earth and his nature is earthy. But that which is born of the Spirit is our human spirit. The second man is of the Spirit and His nature is spiritual and the spiritual nature comes from the Lord of Heaven. Jesus tells us we shouldn't be marveling about the fact that spiritual birth works like natural birth. Just as we had to be born of the flesh before we were ready for earth, even so we must be born of the Spirit of God to become spiritual before we can be ready for Heaven. The way God re-creates us is also similar to the way God created the universe: with His words.

The Two Adams

> And there went out a champion out of the camp of the Philistines, named Goliath, of Gath, whose height was six cubits and a span.

And he had an helmet of brass upon his head, and he was armed with a coat of mail; and the weight of the coat was five thousand shekels of brass. And he had greaves of brass upon his legs, and a target of brass between his shoulders. And the staff of his spear was like a weaver's beam; and his spear's head weighed six hundred shekels of iron: and one bearing a shield went before him. And he stood and cried unto the armies of Israel, and said unto them, Why are ye come out to set your battle in array? am not I a Philistine, and ye servants to Saul? Choose you a man for you, and let him come down to me. If he be able to fight with me, and to kill me, then will we be your servants: but if I prevail against him, and kill him, then shall ye be our servants, and serve us. And the Philistine said, I defy the armies of Israel this day; give me a man, that we may fight together. When Saul and all Israel heard those words of the Philistine, they were dismayed, and greatly afraid. (1 Sam. 17:4-11)

In this passage of scripture with Israel and the Philistines, we see a Bible clue that gives us a picture of the two Adams. This historical event is a picture to us of God's perspective of Adam and Christ as the two Adams, the two heads of the human race. In Eden, Adam was the head of the human race. He was our representative. Whatever happened to Adam would happen to everyone in the human race because we were all in Adam. We are all born as the children of Adam and inherit everything that belongs to Adam. His nature and character are in us all. When Satan came along, Adam was no match for Satan. Satan was the giant to Adam. Adam represented God and God's family. Through obedience to Satan, Adam and all his unborn kids became the slaves of Satan forever.

The armies of Israel were gathered together in battle against the enemies of God. The Philistines stood on one side and the Israelites stood on the other side. It was common practice in those times for armies to send out their champions to battle rather than having the armies do great destruction. Whoever won the fight would win great reward and the army of the champion would become head over the opposing army. The Israelites were God's people. From the eternal perspective, the Philistines represented the enemies of God, which are the people of this world, living by a world system that refuses to recognize God.

The Philistines sent out their champion who would represent the Philistines. He was Goliath, the giant, who was nine feet tall. Just as the devil tempted Jesus for forty days in the wilderness, Goliath taunted the army of Israel for forty days, saying, "Send out your champion to fight against me. I grow lonely out here. If you win we will be your servants, but if I win you shall be our slaves forever." The odds of the Israeli champion were slim. David was just a young man who had been shepherding sheep, but he walked with God. David had experiences with God where beasts had come after his sheep. He slew a bear and a lion with his sling. To a young boy like David, bears and lions were like huge fierce giants. David had learned as a young shepherd boy to protect his flock of sheep from every enemy. When the day came for him to take food to his brothers who were in the army, he was dismayed when he arrived to see the Philistine challenging the armies of God. The men of Israel and King Saul were afraid of Goliath. Yet God was with David and as far as David was concerned, Goliath was no match for God.

You know how a bully picks on someone smaller until he is forced to deal with someone his own size? David knew that Goliath had no covenant with God. When no man would respond to Goliath, David responded. A covenant with God trumped everything, including size. By faith David saw the giant was no match for God. This is a picture of Jesus dealing with Satan on the cross. King Saul tried to give David his own armor, but David saw God as his armor.

> And when the Philistine looked about, and saw David, he disdained him: for he was but a youth, and ruddy, and of a fair countenance. And the Philistine said unto David, Am I a dog that thou comest to me with staves? And the Philistine cursed David by his gods. And the Philistine said to David, Come to me, and I will give thy flesh unto the fowls of the air, and to the beasts of the field. Then said David to the Philistine, Thou comest to me with a sword, and with a spear, and with a shield: but I come to thee in the name of the LORD of hosts, the God of the armies of Israel, whom thou hast defied. This day will the LORD deliver thee into mine hand; and I will smite thee, and take thine head from thee; and I will give the carcasses of the host of the Philistines this day unto the fowls of the air, and to the wild beasts of

the earth; that all the earth may know that there is a God in Israel. And all this assembly shall know that the LORD saveth not with sword and spear: for the battle is the LORD'S, and he will give you into our hands. (1 Sam. 17:42-47)

When David ran toward Goliath, he said, "You come to me with a spear and a shield, but I come to you in the name of the Lord." Goliath was covered in man's armor but David was covered with faith in the covenant of God. Even so Jesus ran from Heaven to Earth and towards Satan for the whole human race, just like David ran toward Goliath for all of Israel. And even though Jesus was all man, He wasn't wearing man's armor. Jesus walked with God and as the champion for the human race, He wore the armor of God.

And it came to pass, when the Philistine arose, and came and drew nigh to meet David that David hasted, and ran toward the army to meet the Philistine. And David put his hand in his bag, and took thence a stone, and slang it, and smote the Philistine in his forehead that the stone sunk into his forehead; and he fell upon his face to the earth. So David prevailed over the Philistine with a sling and with a stone, and smote the Philistine, and slew him; but there was no sword in the hand of David. Therefore David ran, and stood upon the Philistine, and took his sword, and drew it out of the sheath thereof, and slew him, and cut off his head therewith. And when the Philistines saw their champion was dead, they fled. (1 Sam. 17:48-51)

What David did to Goliath hundreds of years before was God's historical demonstration that gives us a mental picture pointing us to what Jesus did to Satan when God raised Him from the dead. God was fulfilling His promise in Genesis 3:15, which says, "I will put enmity between you and her, between your seed and her seed and you will bruise his heel, but he will crush your head."

He that committeth sin is of the devil; for the devil sinneth from the beginning. For this purpose the Son of God was manifested, that he might destroy the works of the devil. (1 John 3:8)

In the Bible, the phrase *the head* represents authority or an authority structure. Here in David, we see the child of God cutting off the head of Goliath the giant. When he did that, all the power of Goliath and the Philistines was gone. In this historical event, God is showing us beforehand a picture of what was going to happen to Satan through the one He has approved to be the King of kings. Just like the Israelites shared in the victory of David over Goliath and the Philistines, even so all believers share in the victory of Jesus over Satan, the god of this world. Satan's authority over God's people is gone. God has kept His promise to all mankind in Adam. God has given us the victory over Satan and his power of death through Christ in us. The victory is yours, if you can believe.

> And you, being dead in your sins and the uncircumcision of your flesh, hath he quickened together with him, having forgiven you all trespasses; Blotting out the handwriting of ordinances that was against us, which was contrary to us, and took it out of the way, nailing it to his cross; And having spoiled principalities and powers, he made a shew of them openly, triumphing over them in it. (Col. 2:13-15)

The Bible says Jesus triumphed over Satan for us and made a show of him and his forces (principalities and powers) in front of all Heaven. As the son of man, Jesus wasn't wearing Adam's armor against Satan. He was wearing the armor of God Himself and He included us in that battle. He was our champion. The Bible says God quickened us together with Christ so that what happened with Christ happened to us. As far as God is concerned we were in Christ when He conquered Satan for us. Now God looks at us and sees we have conquered Satan through Christ in us. That's why the Bible says, "Ye are of God, little children, and have overcome them, because greater is He that is in you than he that is in the world". (1 John 4:4).

> O death, where is thy sting? O grave, where is thy victory? (1 Cor. 15:55)

Jesus is now our King. Satan is still the head of the natural human, but he no longer has any authority over believers in Christ. Satan bruised Jesus' heel, but Jesus crushed Satan's rulership over us. The Bible calls Jesus the head of the body of Christ and the anointing of the head comes down upon the body. The victory of the head belongs to the body. Those who believe in Christ are destined to partake of the victory that was wrought in God by our champion. Jesus has the keys to Death, Hell, and the Grave. Jesus said the gates of Hell shall not prevail against Him and His people. As believers, Satan, with his power of death, is our defeated foe.

> The eyes of your understanding being enlightened; that ye may know what is the hope of his calling, and what the riches of the glory of his inheritance in the saints, And what is the exceeding greatness of his power to us-ward who believe, according to the working of his mighty power, Which he wrought in Christ, when he raised him from the dead, and set him at his own right hand in the heavenly places, Far above all principality, and power, and might, and dominion, and every name that is named, not only in this world, but also in that which is to come: And hath put all things under his feet, and gave him to be the head over all things to the church, Which is his body, the fulness of him that filleth all in all. (Eph. 1:18-23)

The Bible calls Jesus the last Adam. He is the head of a new race. All power in Heaven and Earth has been given unto Him. We can't go to Heaven in the first Adam, but we can go to Heaven in the last Adam. By believing ourselves into Christ we become partakers of His authority. His victory belongs to us and the Bible says *He hath put all things under His feet.* We are partakers of His divine nature and God has destined for us to reign in life by Jesus Christ. The Bible calls us the body of Christ and Jesus is the head of the body. As the body of Christ, all things are under *our* feet.

> God is a Spirit: and they that worship him must worship him in spirit and in truth. (John 4:24)

That which comes first is not spiritual but natural and that which is natural dies. That which comes after is spiritual. You know you were born in the natural man first in order to partake of this natural world. So you should be able to understand that you must be born again of the spiritual man to partake of the spiritual world. Adam was given that opportunity, but he failed to follow God's plan. Adam failed to put on immortality by eating of the Tree of Life. So he and all his offspring have been born under the bondage of sin and death ever since. In Adam we are mere men. Jesus said, *"God is a Spirit and they* that worship him must worship him in Spirit and in Truth."* We can't worship God until we are in the Spirit. We must come to God with brutal honesty and ask Him for His participation in our lives. When we do He gets involved and the only word that we can describe God with is *wonderful.* By coming to God with all our hearts we become spiritual the way we were supposed to be in the beginning. Isn't that wonderful?

> Now this I say, brethren, that flesh and blood cannot inherit the
> kingdom of God; neither doth corruption inherit incorruption.
> (1 Cor. 15:50)

Our earthly nature is natural and not spiritual. Yet in the Bible, through the clues God gives us in the natural, we can understand the spiritual. Corruption cannot inherit incorruption. We must be born of incorruption. Just as the baby is born of the flesh, even so the human spirit must be born again of God's Spirit, or we can't enter into Heaven. God has made this possible through the provision of the last Adam, which is Jesus Christ. It only becomes real to us and for us the moment we believe in Him.

> But now is Christ risen from the dead, and become the firstfruits
> of them that slept. For since by man came death, by man came
> also the resurrection of the dead. For as in Adam all die, even so
> in Christ shall all be made alive. But every man in his own order:
> Christ the firstfruits; afterward they that are Christ's at his coming.
> (1 Cor. 15:20-23)

God created Adam as a living soul, therefore everyone born of Adam is born into earth as living souls. But Jesus is the last Adam, and the Bible says He is a quickening Spirit, and when we come to God through Jesus Christ, God quickens us with His Spirit and we are born again of God. The same Spirit that raised Jesus from the dead quickens us.

For we that are in this tabernacle do groan, being burdened: not for that we would be unclothed, but clothed upon, that mortality might be swallowed up of life. (2 Cor. 5:4)

God doesn't want to cast us out of His universe. God wants to clothe us with Christ and bring us into His eternal home of Heaven. Without being clothed with Christ, we aren't fit for Heaven. It is our inheritance God wants to give us. It's the life we were created to live. A world in which the selfish nature of man is bringing destruction upon the planet and all mankind isn't much to look forward to. If all we have to look forward to is Heaven when we die, but we live like forgiven dogs on earth, we will be most miserable. But that is how many believers live their lives. We think knowledge is what blesses us, but the truth is, knowledge alone without any kind of knowledge of God hurts us. God didn't tell us he who has all the information wins. Learning knowledge may give you a rush or get you a job, or even bring success, but learning without any knowledge of God only deceives us, destroys us and robs us of our eternal inheritance. When it's time to die, knowledge without God won't help you. It will have been a waste of time. Only the knowledge of God will save you then. All through the Bible God has been giving us clues about our eternal inheritance that is laid up for us in Heaven and what life is supposed to be on Earth.

The Two Sons

And if children, then heirs; heirs of God, and joint-heirs with Christ; if so be that we suffer with him, that we may be also glorified to-gether. (Rom. 8:17)

The two Adams have more to do with the two men in whom all men dwell. There are only two men on planet Earth and out of them come all men. In the first man Adam, we are all born of His good and evil nature. In the second man, the last Adam, we are born again of the His divine nature. In the Bible, God demonstrates this fact to us in all the events where we see two sons. In the events of Cain and Abel, Ishmael and Isaac, Jacob and Esau, and even Joseph and his brethren, there is enmity between the natural sons and the spiritual sons. The firstborn always persecutes the second-born because the first man is fighting over the earthly inheritance. If we love the things of this earth more than the things of God, we are still in the first man Adam and not in Christ. The second man loves the things of God, which are eternal. The firstborn and the second-born are also phrases, which imply the same truth.

> Hearken, my beloved brethren, Hath not God chosen the poor of this world rich in faith, and heirs of the kingdom, which he hath promised to them that love him? (Jas. 2:5)

As the heirs of God our real inheritance is eternal. This means we share in the covenant between God and His Son. Jesus died, was buried and rose again to give us a share in His inheritance. The Bible says, if we suffer with Jesus we will also be glorified with Him. How do we share in His sufferings? By dying to the earthly inheritance that we received in Adam to gain the heavenly inheritance that we receive in the last Adam, which is Christ. Every believer goes through the enmity of the two Adams. The first Adam, born of the flesh, the Bible calls the natural man. He is of the earth and his inheritance is earthly. The last Adam, which is Christ, is the spiritual man. The Bible calls him the second man from Heaven. His inheritance is heavenly. God is teaching us in each story of the two sons some aspect of the two spiritual natures and their struggle to possess their inheritance. The struggle in our flesh is the enmity of the two Adams fighting for control of our body so the inheritance can be secured.

> For it is written, that Abraham had two sons, the one by a bond-maid, the other by a freewoman. But he who was of the bond-woman was born after the flesh; but he of the freewoman was by promise. Which things are an allegory: for these are the two covenants; the one from the mount Sinai, which gendereth to bondage, which is Hagar. For this Hagar is mount Sinai in Arabia, and answereth to Jerusalem which now is, and is in bondage with her children. But Jerusalem which is above is free, which is the mother of us all. For it is written, Rejoice, thou barren that bearest not; break forth and cry, thou that travailest not: for the desolate hath

many more children than she which hath an husband. Now we, brethren, as Isaac was, are the children of promise. But as then *he that was born after the flesh persecuted him that was born after the Spirit, even so it is now*. Nevertheless what saith the scripture? Cast out the bondwoman and her son: for the son of the bondwoman shall not be heir with the son of the freewoman. So then, brethren, we are not children of the bondwoman, but of the free. (Gal. 4:22-31)

The Bible is showing us in Ishmael that in our firstborn nature we are born under bondage to the law, which brings us into bondage because the good and evil nature cannot fulfill the law. Therefore, we stand condemned before God and are doomed to die under the penalty of the law. In this world, the law is, the oldest child is the heir of the family. In God's world, even though the firstborn is the heir of this world, he cannot share in the inheritance with the child of promise, who is the second-born. He is the true heir and the true inheritance is eternal life. God is showing us that in Ishmael, who is the firstborn, we will not be heirs of the promise, but rather our inheritance is in Isaac, who is the second-born, the child of promise. We also see with Ishmael and Isaac the fierce enmity between the first-born and the second-born. This enmity continues even until this present day in the Middle East between the natural born sons and the spiritual born sons of Abraham. However, the real lesson for the human race that God wants to teach us in the Bible is the issue of the enmity between the natural man and the spiritual man.

When we see God giving instructions to Moses about the Passover Lamb and He mentions the firstborn of Egypt and the firstborn of Israel, He is talking about the same thing. The firstborn is the natural man in Adam. It is our inheritance of living in this world, which we receive when we are born. The second-born is the spiritual man in Christ. He is the true heir of eternal life, which we receive through the new birth.

When the death angel slew the firstborn of Egypt and passed over the firstborn of Israel, God was showing us how He saves us. Israel became God's firstborn as the blood of the Passover Lamb on their doors preserved them. The blood of Jesus, God's Son, was shed for us so that death might pass over you and make it possible for you to be born of God and become heirs of the heavenly Kingdom. So God was showing us *the natural man* dies as the *spiritual man* is born, and *the new man* is born as the *old man dies*. The new birth is only possible through the innocent sacrificial Lamb of God that would come and die for us, which was Christ. God is hinting to us all throughout the Bible the reality of the new birth.

The Bible says flesh and blood (the firstborn) cannot inherit Heaven and, like Ishmael, must be sent away from the heavenly family. He can only inherit Heaven as he becomes the second-born through the miracle of the new birth. The earthly is not the inheritance, but the heavenly is the true inheritance. The natural man is not the heir of God, but the spiritual man is the true heir of God.

> And *the children struggled together within her*; and she said, If it be so, why am I thus? And she went to enquire of the LORD. And the LORD said unto her, *Two nations* are in thy womb, and two manner of people shall be separated from thy bowels; and the one people shall be stronger than the other people; and *the elder shall serve the younger*. And when her days to be delivered were fulfilled, behold, there were twins in her womb. And the first came out red, all over like an hairy garment; and they called his name Esau. And after that came his brother out, and *his hand took hold on Esau's heel*; and his name was called Jacob: and Isaac was threescore years old when she bare them. (Genesis 25:22-26)

Jacob and Esau are a great example of the birthright and the enmity over the inheritance. The two babies were warring within their mother. Esau was born first and his red color signifies his earthly nature. Jacob came out of the womb right after Esau, holding onto Esau's heel. This event signifies at birth how that which is born first is not spiritual but natural, then afterwards that which is spiritual. Rebekah felt their struggle within her belly and prayed to God about it. God told Rebekah that there were two nations and two manners of people in her womb. God was telling her that the kids in the natural would be two different nations (families), but they would also have two different spiritual natures. One would love earthly things and the other would love spiritual things. That is exactly how the events of Jacob and Esau unfold. Esau was born first so he was the natural heir of the family. But God says the true inheritance is spiritual and the second-born (Jacob) who lives for the eternal inheritance is the true heir of God.

Jacob and Esau fought over the inheritance as they were coming out of the womb. God was showing us there is always a fight between the first-born and the second-born. God formed Adam (the human body) out of the dust of the ground. Your body is your own real estate, made of earth, which you received by natural birth. Your body is the heir of this world and earth is your earthly inheritance. It has been in control of you all your life and when you receive God's spirit, your body will continue to fight for control of you, but your body is not your true inheritance. God created you for Heaven. Your true inheritance is spiritual. Your spirit is able to bring your body under control so you can walk with the heavenly Father.

God also said to Rebekah about Jacob and Esau, there are two peoples in your womb and the elder shall serve the younger. God uses this event as a mental picture, saying to us, just as there were two nations and peoples in her womb, even so there are two natures in each human, by two births, with two different inheritances and the elder (the firstborn) shall serve the younger (the second-born). That process of the firstborn and the second-born fighting for the rulership goes on in us after we are born again. I discussed the firstborn and the second-born in the section about the Passover lamb. Now I will go into more detail from the Bible perspective. The firstborn is our bodies. He is our inheritance from Adam. The second-born is our re-created spirits. He is our inheritance from Christ, the last Adam. God gives us a new spirit (His Spirit) when we are born again. Once, our bodies ruled us, and now, after the new birth, our spirits rule over our bodies and our body (the elder) is to serve our spirit (the younger). What we got in the first birth (soul and body) serves what we get in the second birth (the re-created human spirit). In this way the elder is serving the younger. After the new birth, the war between our body and our spirit continues until our body begins to serve our spirit.

The same principle of the enmity can be seen with the life of Joseph. He is the miracle child of Jacob and is persecuted by his brothers, but God exalts him as the true heir of all things, which points us to Jesus. The new birth is what the Bible is all about, because through the new birth we receive our spiritual inheritance. The new birth is the door into son-ship with God the heavenly Father.

And if children, then heirs; *heirs of God, and joint-heirs with Christ*;
if so be that we suffer with him, that we may be also glorified
together. For I reckon that the sufferings of this present time
are not worthy to be compared with the glory which shall be
revealed in us. For the earnest expectation of the creature wait-
eth for the manifestation of the sons of God. For the creature
was made subject to vanity, not willingly, but by reason of him
who hath subjected the same in hope, Because the creature itself also shall be delivered from the bondage of corruption into
the glorious liberty of the children of God. For we know that the
whole creation groaneth and travaileth in pain together until now.
(Rom. 8:17-22)

The inheritance God gives us as the second-born is eternal and Jesus is
the example of what it looks like. For too long the heirs of God have been
living beneath their privileges as they walk through this world. Son-ship is
the doctrine we haven't heard taught much in the church. Son-ship is what
all creation is groaning to see. While the race and the planet are under the
threat of destruction at the hands of greedy, evil men, the universe wants to
be fully redeemed from the curse, liberated from the powers of Satan, and
restored in its relationship with God, to enjoy the true inheritance we were
created for.

Nevertheless, what saith the scripture? Cast out the bondwoman
and her son: for the son of the bondwoman shall not be heir with
the son of the freewoman. (Gal. 4:30)

We all want to live forever. God created us to live forever, but eternal
life only comes through the new birth, the rebirth of the human spirit.
This only God can do. This God is pleased to do. The moment we believe
in Jesus Christ, God quickens our spirits and we are born again. Have you
been born of God yet? Your inheritance is laid up for you. You can know
how these things can be. God is waiting for you to receive your inheritance
as you come to Him by Jesus Christ. It doesn't matter what color you are or
what culture you are from. All of creation is waiting for you to become an
heir of God. The Bible says the angels rejoice when you become an heir of

God. Just like God clothed Adam and Eve, God wants to clothe you with Jesus Christ so your death can be swallowed up in His life.

Man Shall Not Live by Bread Alone

> But he answered and said, It is written, Man shall not live by bread alone, but by every word that proceedeth out of the mouth of God. (Matt. 4:4)

> Now ye are clean through the word which I have spoken unto you. (John 15:3)

Just like we must eat food in the natural so we can grow and mature and become complete, even so we must eat spiritual food in order to be born again of God's Spirit, grow, mature, and become complete in Christ. Jesus said God's spiritual food comes to us in His words. Just as God spoke words and the worlds were created, even so God speaks words to us and the life-giving power of God's Spirit comes out of His words and quickens us in our hearts. Jesus called the words of God seeds. He said, just like seeds go down into the ground and sprout up with new life, even so the words of God come into our hearts and make us alive with God's Spirit. The words of God come to open our eyes so we can see truth. As we embrace the truth with our hearts, His Spirit quickens us and makes us alive unto God. The life nature of Heaven is in Jesus, the Son of God. God puts deposits of His life into us by His words. Just like God created the natural worlds by words, Jesus is saying the life that is from above comes when the human hears the words of God and understands them with his heart. The Spirit of God contained in the words of God from the lips of Jesus quickens the human spirit and he is born again of God. Jesus said, "That which is born of the flesh is our flesh and that which is born of the Spirit is our spirits."

> It is the spirit that quickeneth; the flesh profiteth nothing: the words that I speak unto you, they are spirit, and they are life. (John 6:63)

He also said, "Don't marvel that I'm telling you that you must be born again." Jesus tries to help Nicodemus out by saying ". . . those that are born of the Spirit are like the wind. You can feel the effects and see the effects but you can't tell where their power is coming from or where it's going." So Nicodemus responds again with one of my favorite unanswered questions, "How can these things be?" Jesus sounds perplexed, saying to Nicodemus, "Aren't you a master in Israel and you don't know these things?"

A master in his day was like a PhD and a doctor of divinity in our day. Then Jesus goes on to say, "We speak what we know and we testify to what we've seen, but you don't receive our witness." This means God and His Son are talking with Him, speaking the words of God to a master of Israel and he still isn't getting a witness from the Spirit of God like He is supposed to. Part of the quickening of the Spirit in our hearts is the witness. We know God has revealed something to us because there is witness from God inside our hearts confirming what we know. It's sort of like our conscience, but the witness is greater than our conscience.

Nicodemus was showing a hard head, but the fact that he is there talking with Jesus shows that God is working in his heart, just like God should be working in your heart right now. Then Jesus said, "If I tell you of earthly things and you won't believe, how will you believe when I tell you of heavenly things?" This is a principle of revelation that God uses besides His words. God works in the natural to demonstrate the spiritual. The Old Testament is full of earthly events that become mental pictures, which symbolize heavenly truths. In this case with Nicodemus, Jesus is using childbirth to symbolize the rebirth of the human spirit. Then Jesus says, "And no man hath ascended up to heaven, but he that came down from heaven, even the Son of man, *which is in heaven.*" Jesus is telling us that no natural man is going to ascend to Heaven, but only the one that came down from Heaven and He is the one who has *Heaven in Him.* Everywhere Jesus went God was with Him. So He was literally walking in Heaven on Earth when He walked in the presence of God. That is the life He came to give us. Jesus taught and demonstrated what eternal life is. It is the heavenly Father and His sons walking together forever. Now you may think walking with God is religion, but God is fully able and willing to manifest Himself unto you, if your heart is right. God gets pleasure walking with His kids just like normal parents get pleasure being with their kids. That is not religion.

> Fear not, little flock; for it is your Father's good pleasure to give you the kingdom. (Luke 12:32)

We deceive ourselves all the time, but we can't fool God. He knows when you are coming to Him with all your heart and when you do He will respond to you. If you come to God with all your heart, you will be born again of the Spirit of God and you will know you are a child of God and that you are going to Heaven when you die. That is what God wants, and that is really what we want. But we have to get beyond all the silly deceptions we believe about ourselves and get to the place where we are honest with God and serious about our eternal destiny. God gives us all the same choice He gave Adam and Eve. We can follow His instructions and live forever or we can go our own way and be lost forever.

You can make that decision right now. You can come to God right now in your heart and you can speak words out loud to God and He will respond to your heart. God isn't a thought, an imagination, or a religion. God is a person just like you are a person and He wants to have a relationship with you more than you want to have a relationship with Him. If you call out to God for real, He will answer you and save you. It's like if you have a pain in your heart and you think you're dying and you cry out, "Help, save me." When our heart is in pain spiritually and we truly call upon God, He hears us and answers us, and we become born again. That's why God sent Jesus from Heaven to Earth that we might not perish but have eternal life.

> And as Moses lifted up the serpent in the wilderness, even so must the Son of man be lifted up: That whosoever believeth in him should not perish, but have eternal life. For God so loved the world, that he gave his only begotten Son, that whosoever believeth in him should not perish, but have everlasting life. (John 3:14-16)

Finally, Jesus said to Nicodemus, "For God so loved the world, that he gave His only begotten Son, that whosoever believeth in Him should not perish, but have everlasting life." This is the heart of the Bible. God wants us all to live. God doesn't want anyone to perish for eternity. Those who know not that God is love are missing out on truth and life. Everything God does is a manifestation of love. Everything God does gives life. God so loved that He created the universe and God so loved that He gave us His Son. That's what love does; it gives to the one loved. What did God give? He gave us His best. He gave us His Son. He gave up His Son for us to die that we might live. If we knew what love is and how love comes from God, we would jump at the invitation to fellowship with God, but we are so deceived we think God is a religion and who wants some old dead cold religion? God knows we cannot live by bread alone. Physical life is only part of spiritual life. God knows without His love we cannot live forever. God has overcome the death problem for us through His Son because He wants us to live forever with Him in Heaven. Here is how God so loved us.

> For when *we were yet without strength*, in due time *Christ died for the ungodly*. For scarcely for a righteous man will one die: yet peradventure for a good man some would even dare to die. But *God commendeth his love toward us*, in that, *while we were yet sinners*, Christ died for us. Much more then, being now justified by his blood, we shall be saved from wrath through him. For if, when *we were enemies, we were reconciled to God* by the death of his Son, much more, being reconciled, *we shall be saved by his life*. And not only so, but we also joy in God through our Lord Jesus Christ, by whom we have now received the atonement. (Rom. 5:6-11)

When We Were Without Strength

That means we can't save ourselves and we can't be good enough. We can't do enough good works to make up for our bad deeds. Besides that, we like doing bad deeds. We like lust and deception and all the corruption of the human heart. When the human truly comes to God, he doesn't like all that and he cries to God to be delivered from all that and God gladly saves him.

While We Were Yet Sinners

God saves us the moment we call to Him, even while we are sinners. The moment you cry out to God He is there ready to deliver you from death. God doesn't care about all the evil you have done. He knows when your heart truly changes and He quickens you, that you will be born again and become His very own child.

When We Were Enemies

Yes, we even dislike talking about religion and spiritual things. We hate it. God knows all that. We were born that way. That is why we need to be born again. Once we are born again we don't hate the things of God anymore. That is one of the ways we know we are truly born again. No, we will never be perfect in this life. God doesn't ask us to be perfect. Why is it unbelievers demand perfection of believers when it's okay for them to not be perfect? No human can ever be perfect. So get over it. God doesn't demand perfection from anyone, so why should you? All God asks is that you become honest with yourself and come to Him with your heart so you might not perish, but have everlasting life.

God So Loved

God so loved us when we were without strength, while we were yet sinners and when we were enemies. John 3:16 says God so loved us that He gave His only begotten Son that *whosoever believeth in Him might not perish*, but have everlasting life. Jesus said, while they were nailing the nails through His hands, "Father, forgive them for they know not what they do." Love like that has never been seen before, but only with the Son of God. Everything Jesus did, He did out of love for you. If you think it's impossible for God to love you then you are wrong. God has already loved you. God so loved you before you were born. Have you responded to His love? Will you pray to Him now with your heart? The Bible says you shall be saved by His life.

A New Species of Being

> Therefore, if any man be in Christ, he is a new creature: *old things are passed away*; behold, all things are become new. And all things are of God, who hath reconciled us to himself by Jesus Christ, and hath given to us the ministry of reconciliation. (2 Cor. 5:17-18)

> In Christ Jesus neither circumcision nor uncircumcision avails anything, but a new creation. (Gal. 6:15)

Receiving Christ is the only way God can give us His Spirit, which has the natural tendency to want to do right and avoid doing wrong. Through the new birth we are born into God's family and this is how we come into right relationship with God. This is how we receive the nature of Christ. This is what it means for a person to be born again. He will never be perfect in this world, but he will resemble Jesus. Just like we are born into this see and be seen world, we are also born again into God's spiritual kingdom where Jesus is King.

We are all going to live forever because God, who is a Spirit, created us as spirit beings, in His image and likeness. Where we're going to spend eternity is up to us. By receiving Christ, the heavenly Father activates the experience of Christ into our hearts and we become a new species of being that never existed before. The hidden man of the heart is brand new and is the very same Spirit of Christ. With Christ's Spirit in us, God looks at our hearts and sees we have died on the cross, and have been raised from the dead, and are now seated together with Christ in heavenly places (see Eph. 1:3). The same spirit that went through that whole process now dwells in us. God looks at us and declares us as righteous as Jesus is and He loves us as much as Jesus, because the greater one dwells in us.

> For ye are all the children of God by faith in Christ Jesus. For as many of you as have been baptized into Christ have put on Christ. There is neither Jew nor Greek, there is neither bond nor free, there is neither male nor female: for ye are all one in Christ Jesus. And if ye be Christ's, then are ye Abraham's seed, and heirs according to the promise. (Gal. 3:26-29)

In God's world every life matters. There is no sex, no color, no culture or political affiliation with God. The deceptions of the flesh have no power with God. There is no difference with God between anyone, but all have the same inheritance of eternal life and access to the heavenly Father. There are different rewards for those who walk with the Father but His love is the same for us all. God wants to see you in Heaven but He leaves the choice up to you. Your decision about where you are going to spend eternity is the most important decision you will ever make, but there's much more to God's gift of eternal life than just going to Heaven when you die. As intelligent as man may be, with the sin nature and the self program, the Bible calls him a beast in God's sight. God has offered the gift of eternal life to every soul ever born of Adam. He has sent His only Son from Heaven to make eternal life possible for us. Those of us who believe in Christ are a new species of being that never existed before. We are a new race made up of all cultures and peoples. The Bible says, in Christ there is neither Jew nor Greek, there is neither bond nor free, there is neither male nor female, but we are a new species of being that never existed before. Our citizenship is now in Heaven. This is the secret of eternity.

But God has much more in store for us than just forgiveness of sins and Heaven. If I forgive you of something, then you are released from the sin you committed against me. That doesn't mean you have stopped hating me. It also doesn't mean we have a relationship. It means you are forgiven and now you have the opportunity and potential of having a relationship with me. You still must change your attitude and overcome your hatred against me. You also must do mutual things with me that prove we have a relationship. Forgiveness of sins puts you back into the same position Adam was in with God and with the same potential. God is saying in the Bible, "I've done everything necessary for you to know me and love me. Now you can walk with me in friendship and love and become a part of my heavenly family if you so choose."

I hope you make the right choice. If you haven't already, I hope you will look up to Heaven where your help comes from and cry out to God with all your heart and let God touch you. He wants to save you forever. The moment you believe in the Son of God, you will obtain a witness from God, just like Abel, that you are righteous in His sight and you now belong to Him.

Pray to God

> That if thou shalt confess with thy mouth the Lord Jesus, and shalt believe in thine heart that God hath raised him from the dead, thou shalt be saved. For with the heart man believeth unto righteousness; and with the mouth confession is made unto salvation. (Rom. 10:9)

If you've never experienced the goodness of God, right now you can pray and receive Christ into your heart by faith. God has promised that when you pray and receive Jesus, He will pour out His Spirit upon you and you will be born again and become a child of God. Jesus wants to save you and have a relationship with you just like He did with people in the Bible. His supernatural power is the same today as it was when He walked the earth. God did everything He did to save you from death and He will activate His gift of eternal life in your heart the moment you ask Him to.

> Behold, I stand at the door, and knock: if any man hear my voice, and open the door, *I will come in to him, and will sup with him, and he with me.* To him that overcometh will I grant to sit with me in my throne, even as I also overcame, and am set down with my Father on his throne. He that hath an ear, let him hear what the Spirit saith unto the churches. (Rev. 3:20-22)

Jesus is standing at the door of your heart right now. Just be honest with God and pray from your heart. For me it was telling God, I don't want to die, but I want to live and learn the *Truth of Eternity*. Jesus responded to me. He knew I was real and I knew He was real. For you it may just be inviting Jesus into your heart. But you must speak words and you must believe. You could say words similar to this:

Heavenly Father,

I understand I was born into planet Earth as a sinner, a child of Adam, without God, without hope in the world and headed for Hell. I realize you are the only one that can save me. I understand I don't deserve salvation, nor can I earn salvation, but you offer it to me as the gift of God through Jesus Christ. Thank you for making provision for me. Thank you for giving your Son for me so I might live forever with you. I come to you with my Passover Lamb (Jesus). I accept Jesus as my Lord and Savior. I receive forgiveness of all my sins and believe you have raised Jesus from the dead. I ask you to save me now, to become my heavenly Father and to give me the Spirit of your Son. I ask in Jesus' name.

> Verily, verily, I say unto you, He that heareth my word, and believeth on him that sent me, hath everlasting life, and shall not come into condemnation; but is passed from death unto life. (John 5:24)

Jesus,

Thank you for laying down your life for me that I might live forever in Heaven with you. Thank you for loving me before I was born. I open the door of my heart and ask you to come into my life. I receive you as my Lord and Savior and I believe God has reconciled me to Himself through your death upon the cross. I ask you now to save me and fill me with your Spirit. I now choose to receive your Spirit and be born again. With all my heart I open the door of my heart and I believe I receive your gift of eternal life now. Amen.

> For whosoever shall call upon the name of the Lord shall be saved. (Rom. 10:13)

> But what saith it? The word is nigh thee, even in thy mouth, and in thy heart: that is, the word of faith, which we preach; That *if thou shalt confess with thy mouth* the Lord Jesus, and *shalt believe in thine heart* that God hath raised him from the dead, thou shalt be saved. For with the heart man believeth unto righteousness; and with the mouth confession is made unto salvation. For the scripture saith, Whosoever believeth on him shall not be ashamed. (Rom. 10:8-11)

I've fed you bread and water. Bread and water is for unbelievers. I've also fed you milk and milk is for believers. If you have invited Jesus into your life, the Bible says you are a new creature. God heard your prayer and He will never let you go. This book has provided you with a foundation so you can understand the Bible for yourself. Now it is time to feed you with some meat. As you go into the next chapter, be strong and believe that the Spirit of God is now quickening your heart and believe you have passed from death to life. Believe that you are becoming born again through Christ in you. As you believe, realize you are pleasing God. The Bible says, without faith it is impossible to please God. Remember the true goal of the Bible is, you can be a son (of God).

Personal Study Notes

CHAPTER 9

YOU
Can Be a
SON

Behold, what manner of love the Father
hath bestowed upon us, that we should be called
the sons of God.

1 JOHN 3:1

The True Incentive of the Bible

> But now is Christ risen from the dead, and become the firstfruits of them that slept. For since by man came death, by man came also the resurrection of the dead. For as in Adam all die, even so in Christ shall all be made alive. (1 Cor. 15:20-22)

Now that you have learned about the operation of God and the new birth, you can understand *God's purpose* for creation and the *true incentive* of the Bible. He who created us is re-creating us as His very own children, to be citizens of Heaven and to be the lights of the world. No religion can even come close. The only thing religion does is cause the human to focus on himself, but there is no power for the human in any religion to change the human nature of self. Man can never become a god. As much as man wants to be his own god, man can never ascend, achieve, or attain to a level of god-hood.

> But God, who is rich in mercy, for his great love wherewith he loved us, Even when *we were dead* in sins, hath quickened us together with Christ, (by grace ye are saved;) And *hath raised us up together*, and *made us sit together* in heavenly places in Christ Jesus: That in the ages to come he might shew the exceeding riches of his grace in his kindness toward us through Christ Jesus. For *by grace are ye saved through faith*; and that not of yourselves: *it is the gift of God*: Not of works, lest any man should boast. For we are his workmanship, created in Christ Jesus unto good works, which God hath before ordained that we should walk in them. (Eph. 2:4-10)

We were all born in Adam and we never made it to the next phase of spiritual growth by eating of the Tree of Life. In the natural man Adam, we all die, but the *Good News* of the Bible is God has provided a way for us to get out of death and into life. Jesus is the way. It's by grace (the goodness of God) through faith (believing God's word) we put on immortality (Christ in us). God sent His Son from Heaven to Earth to become the Son of man that all who believe in Him might be born again of His divine nature and become the sons of God. This is the secret of eternity. God isn't just saving us. God isn't just having a family. God isn't just having children. God is having more sons. God had one Son and He wanted more. Just like in the Garden Adam was our life, even so as believers *our life is now hid with Christ in God*. When we come to God through Jesus Christ, God activates in our hearts what happened from the cross to the throne, where God took us out of Adam and put us into Christ, and we become born again of God. Jesus becomes our example of son-ship. Jesus taught and demonstrated to us that we can accomplish son-ship as we live by His measure of faith.

> Likewise reckon ye also yourselves to be dead indeed unto sin, but alive unto God through Jesus Christ our Lord. (Rom. 6:11)

Yes, we are dead to sin, but the good news is we are alive unto God through Christ in us. The life God originally created us to have is in Christ. When we come to God, He puts us into Christ just like He originally put us into Adam, and we are born again and made alive unto Him by the Spirit of God. Through the new birth we become citizens of Heaven. Life then becomes the process of learning to *live by Jesus* and mature into the sons of God on earth. You can see the grace of God goes far beyond the wonderful provision of the forgiveness of sins and Heaven when we die. Jesus didn't leave Heaven and come to Earth just to show off. Jesus didn't just come to tell us He was the Son of God. Jesus came to earth to destroy him that has the power of death, that is the devil, so we could enter into His life. What that means to us is far beyond all that we can think or imagine. It is supernatural. God did everything He did, Jesus did everything He did and the Holy Spirit is now doing everything He does to give us the power to become the sons of God. Many will settle for forgiveness of sins and Heaven when they die. That is the glorious provision of the cross. What Jesus did has canceled our sins, reconciled us unto God and has purchased for us everlasting life. Just thinking about the fact that we are free of God's judgment and condemnation forever is enough to establish peace in our hearts. However, the resurrection of Jesus has endowed us with the life from above that empowers us into son-ship. What brings God the greatest glory is having more sons. God is glorified when we grow up into Him in all things.

The Life That Was Promised

In hope of eternal life, which God, that cannot lie, promised before the world began. (Titus 1:2)

God promised us eternal life before creation. God offered us eternal life in the Garden of Eden, but man turned away from the life to walk by the beat of a different drummer. Adam made the wrong decision. His decision affected the whole race within him and it affected all of creation. Imagine if you were in his position, in a Garden of Paradise, and whatever you decide will affect the whole race of your unborn children. Your decision will affect their eternal destiny. We all do that to some degree every day. Everything you do affects somebody, including your children. Every choice you make is an example to somebody.

And this is the promise that he hath promised us, even eternal life. (1 John 2:25)

Your lifestyle is guiding somebody. You can't live in this world without affecting somebody. Have you ever done something that affected somebody else in a bad way? Imagine how Adam felt. God purposed for us to live and not die. But the decision to walk in God's kind of life belonged to the creature. God knew what Adam's decision would be. Yet God still created Adam in His own image and likeness, and gave him the freedom to make his own decisions and determine his own eternal destiny. Even so, God has given you the freedom to make your own decisions and determine your own eternal destiny. God planned all along to make it possible for us to have the life that was promised. God even trusted Adam to make the right decision like a good son. Adam's choices affected you and me in a negative way. Jesus' choices affect you and me in a positive way. Adam's failure is a major part of the lesson of the Bible. Hopefully you will learn much from his failure.

And this is the record that God hath given to us eternal life, and this life is in his Son. He that hath the Son hath life; and he that hath not the Son of God hath not life. (1 John 5:11-12)

If you have the Son in you, then you have the life. If you don't have the Son in you, then you don't have the life that was promised. What does that mean? It means that just as Adam's way of living life without God was in us, even so when we come to God through Jesus Christ, His way of life, the life that was promised, is in us now.

The Life That Was Manifested

But as many as received him, *to them gave the power to become the sons of God*, even to them that believe on his name: Which were born, not of blood, nor of the will of the flesh, nor of the will of man, but of God. (John 1:12-13)

God has given us the power to become the sons of God. That means you can walk in the same fellowship with the heavenly Father as Jesus does. You can live the same lifestyle Jesus lives. You can partake of His divine nature and experience the same results Jesus has by living the lifestyle of the Son through Christ in you. It is the Father's good pleasure to give us the kingdom.

That which was from the beginning, which we have heard, which we have seen with our eyes, which we have looked upon, and our hands have handled, of the Word of life; For the life was manifested, and we have seen it, and bear witness, and shew unto you that eternal life, which was with the Father, and was manifested unto us. (1 John 1:1-2)

The son is the heir of God and His inheritance is the life that was promised to us before creation. Adam lost our inheritance but Jesus brought our inheritance of eternal life back to us. The lifestyle of eternity is the lifestyle Jesus taught and demonstrated unto us as He walked with God. God is the heavenly Father and we are His offspring. Ultimately you can be a son. As in the natural, so it is also in the spiritual. You can be a son, destined for eternity with the Father, but it takes time to mature.

Growing Up into Him

> In that hour Jesus rejoiced in the Spirit and said, "I thank You, Father, Lord of heaven and earth, that You have hidden these things from the wise and prudent and revealed them to babes. Even so, Father, for so it seemed good in Your sight. (Luke 10:21 NKJV)

If you have been born again of the Spirit of God, you are destined for sonship. Just like in the natural you were a babe when you were born, even so it is in the spiritual. The Bible calls us *babes in Christ* after the new birth. The new birth is the rebirth of the human spirit and it is just as real of a birth as natural childbirth. Just as in the natural you grew up as a child and were corrected by your parents, even so it is in the spiritual. You grow up as a child of God with God's parental correction. Having God as your parent is just as real as having human parents. Just as in the natural you matured and became an adult son or daughter of your parents, able to carry on the family business, even so in the spiritual you mature and progress spiritually and God calls you a son. God isn't just having babes. God isn't just having children. God is having sons. God is enlarging His heavenly family.

It's not about being perfect or living a perfect life. It never was. It's about walking with God and loving God forever. That's the way it began in the Garden of Eden, that's the way it was with Jesus, and that's the way it will end. In the book of Revelation, we see the end of all things and what we see is the Father and His heavenly family. And the Tree of Life is the only tree that is left. The curse upon the planet and Satan's dominion of death over the human race only began when man joined Satan and his agenda and separated from God. However, God's plan to enlarge His heavenly family with many more sons isn't dependent upon the creature or the race but upon the power of God. Death is no match for God and Satan is no match for the Son of God. All the fathers and patriarchs walked with God and experienced God's super on their natural. The Bible says they are examples and witnesses unto us upon whom the end of the worlds is come. Just as Jesus was born supernaturally by the power of God, even so we are born again supernaturally by the power of God. Just as Jesus grew and matured, even so God's children must grow and mature in their relationship with God, which the Bible calls godliness. The sons of God will inherit glory, and God's purpose to enlarge his heavenly family will be fulfilled.

> Forasmuch then as we are the offspring of God, we ought not to think that the Godhead is like unto gold, or silver, or stone, graven by art and man's device. And the times of this ignorance God winked at; but now commandeth all men everywhere to repent: Because he hath appointed a day, in the which he will judge the world in righteousness by that man whom he hath ordained; whereof he hath given assurance unto all men, in that he hath raised him from the dead. (Acts 17:29-31)

Marriage is God's original example of spiritual maturity. Two become one as they repent of living for self by intimately learning about each other and changing to fit each other. I have learned much wisdom from my wife, Bonnie. She is a godly woman who has suffered much on behalf of loving others. She demands wisdom in life. She demands love and actions that demonstrate love. Marriages and families are immature until parents are humbled to please their mates and love their kids. Growing a marriage requires getting the *self out* and the *love in*. Each spouse must do things to please the other until each spouse becomes the life of the other. A godly marriage isn't just signing a piece of paper so people can live together and be roommates and help each other pay the bills. In the same way, God expects us to repent and draw near to Him, to get the death out and the life in, so we can have fellowship with Him.

God did what we needed done to make it possible for us to become His children. He expects us to do our part, to change our hearts and minds and be reconciled unto God so we can fulfill our eternal destiny in Heaven with Him forever. Comprehending God's program will take a lifetime, but our life on earth is only a few moments in eternity. God has historically proven to us that His program works. God has shown us that the power of God flows through His Son and as His offspring we are destined to become like Him. Death has been defeated for us. We have become united to Him and have put on immortality. In the blink of an eye we shall enter into eternity, but while we live on planet Earth, God expects us to mature in His divine nature and to bring others into the light.

Spiritual Maturity

Spiritual Maturity from Darkness to Light

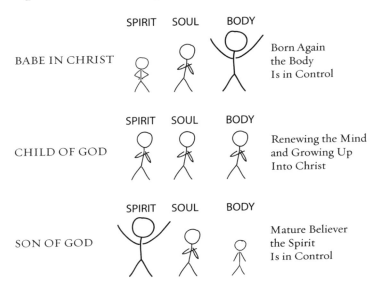

There are three levels of faith in the Bible: the babe, the child, and the son. In each level, I will make a statement that describes the level of mental understanding in each point of spiritual growth. Then I will give a few scriptures to support the statement and then I will elaborate with confessions. As you read these confessions, hopefully you can be able to see these spiritual transitions taking place in yourselves.

1. Babes in Christ

I'm a new creature in Christ Jesus. I was in Adam and now *I am in Christ* and God is now my heavenly father.

> Therefore if any man be in Christ, he *is* a new creature: old things *are* passed away; behold, all things *are* become new. And all things *are* of God, who *hath* reconciled us to himself by Jesus Christ, and *hath* given to us the ministry of reconciliation. (2 Cor. 5:17-18)

I am learning that God loves me and He is my heavenly Father. I know I'm a new creature in Christ Jesus, that old things have passed away and all things have become new. I am learning all the promises of God and I understand I am forgiven of all my sins. I realize in Adam we all die, but the Son of God died on the cross for me to be my Lamb of God and bear away my sins, making it possible for me to be born again and to come back to God.

> As newborn babes, desire the sincere milk of the word that ye may grow thereby. (1 Pet. 2:2)

As a babe everything is new to me. I believe my sins are gone. I understand God is my very own Father and I am His very own child. I understand the newfound truth that I am in the family of God, and that I am going to Heaven when I die. Jesus is my Savior and I know He loves me. I am learning about all the promises of God. These are some of the first spiritual concepts of faith that belong to the newborn creature. While I am a babe in Christ I make all kinds of mistakes just like natural babies do.

> And I, brethren, could not speak unto you as unto spiritual, but as unto carnal, even as unto babes in Christ. (1 Cor. 3:1)

Babies do things wrong naturally. They have to be trained to do things right. That's human nature. Newborns have no understanding of what they are doing and parents have to teach them and keep them under control for their own good. It's a lot of work, but it's worth the energy. Even so this passage of scripture says babes are still carnal and can't handle deep spiritual truth. If you feed meat to a baby it will choke. Feeding spiritual babes deep truths will do the same. Babes must be taught who they are in Christ and what belongs to them. It is a lot of work, but coming to know God as your parent is something that will take *time* to learn.

> Verily I say unto you, Whosoever shall not receive the kingdom of God as a little child shall in no wise enter therein. (Luke 18:17)

2. Children of God

Adam was in me and now *Christ is being formed in me* and I can be a son. I want to know my heavenly father.

> For ye are all the children of God by faith in Christ Jesus. (Gal. 3:26)

> Now we, brethren, as Isaac was, are the children of promise. (Gal. 4:28)

I am learning that God is my heavenly Father, that He loves me and meets all my needs according to His riches in glory by Christ Jesus who now lives in me. I am learning the promises of God and I believe that I am forgiven of all my sins, I am going to Heaven when I die and now I walk with God in my life. I believe God's testimony in the books of Galatians and Ephesians, which says, I was a sinner in Adam and I was an heir of Adam's judgment and eternal destiny. The Bible says I was without hope, a child of wrath, without God in the world, worthy of death. I realize in Adam we all die, but the Son of God died on the cross for me to be my Lamb of God and bear away my sins. God spiritually put me in Christ on the cross, where I was crucified with Him, buried with Him, punished for my sins, raised from the dead, and I am now seated together with Him in heavenly places in Christ Jesus. Through the new birth I have been made alive unto God in the last Adam, Jesus Christ. Now I walk in newness of life and I am witnessing that God walks with me, corrects me, instructs me and is pleased with me. Now the promise of the Spirit is son-ship and fellowship with God.

> My little children, of whom I travail in birth again until Christ be formed in you. (Gal. 4:19)

Now in Christ I have eternal life. I have believed the words of Jesus and I have been born again of God. I believe God's testimony in the books of Romans and Corinthians, which says I am a new species of being in Christ Jesus and God is now forming Christ in me. I am growing up into Him and God is now my very own Father. I can walk with God as though I've never sinned and I'm not just a sinner with a Christian label. The Bible says, "as He is so am I in this present world." Yet I see sin is still fighting within me to bring me back into bondage to the corruption of lust that I used to enjoy as a child of Adam.

> I beseech you therefore, brethren, by the mercies of God, that ye present your bodies a living sacrifice, holy, acceptable unto God, which is your reasonable service. And be not conformed to this world: but be ye transformed by the renewing of your mind, that ye may prove what is that *good*, and *acceptable*, and *perfect*, will of God. (Rom. 12:1-2)

I don't like sinning and I am learning the way of the Spirit that empowers me to overcome sin. Even though I am born again and have no past with God, sin still takes advantage of me and makes me look like a sinner. But I know the blood of Jesus was shed for me and that I am a child of God because His Spirit bears witness with my spirit that I am His very own child. I am destined to overcome all that I inherited in Adam so I can live by Jesus Christ. Son-ship pleases the Father and satisfies me, the human.

3. Sons of God

Christ is in me now by His Spirit and through Christ in me I walk with the heavenly Father and I am a son.

> Behold, what manner of love the Father hath bestowed upon us, that we should be called the sons of God: therefore the world knoweth us not, because it knew him not. Beloved, now are we the sons of God, and it doth not yet appear what we shall be: but we know that, when he shall appear, we shall be like him; for we shall see him as he is. (1 John 3:1-2)

I am learning to walk in my inheritance as an heir of God. He is teaching me by His word and guiding me by His Spirit in life. I understand that Christ is in me now. I am learning to live by Him and His divine nature is growing in me. My attitudes are changing, my ways are changing and I can see God demonstrating His presence in my life. The Father fills me with His Spirit so I can be like Jesus and walk in fellowship with Him. I am learning to do nothing without the Father and the Father shows me what to do that pleases Him. I see sin as an obstacle and I work to overcome the nature of the flesh in every way. I no longer follow the paths of the world and I can see that God is actively involved in all my affairs. My goal is to use my faith to overcome everything I inherited in the first Adam that I might walk in the divine nature of Jesus Christ, the last Adam.

> But he that doeth truth cometh to the light, that his deeds may be made manifest, that they are wrought in God. (John 3:21)

I believe I am becoming a fully grown Son of God as I learn to *live by Jesus*. I believe God's testimony which says, I can have the same relationship with the heavenly Father that Jesus has. I can live the same life Jesus lived and experience the same results Jesus did through Christ in me. Jesus said the works He does I will do also. Nothing is impossible for me, as I believe through Christ in me. I now walk with the heavenly Father and my purpose is to do nothing of self, but only what I see my Father doing. I now partake of His divine nature. I now hate the natural things that I once loved and I love the spiritual things that I once hated. I desire to see Jesus in me. I am learning to *only be led of the Spirit of Christ in me*.

> For as many as are led by the Spirit of God, they are the sons of God. (Rom. 8:14)

I purpose in my heart to prove all things and overcome all things that used to dominate me in Adam. I take up my cross in Christ and lay down my life in Adam that I might take it up again through Christ in me. I walk in the light and do the truth. I depart from evil that all my deeds may become manifest that they are being wrought in God.

> Beloved, now are we the sons of God, and it doth not yet appear what we shall be: but we know that, when he shall appear, we shall be like him; for we shall see him as he is. (1 John 3:2)

My future experience is the fruit of a now experience. Faith is always now. God calls me a son now because He knows how I am going to be when He is finished with me. Even though God calls me a son now, I am not perfect and don't know what I shall be but I know I will be like Him.

> That ye may be blameless and harmless, the sons of God, without rebuke, in the midst of a crooked and perverse nation, among whom ye shine as lights in the world. (Phil. 2:15)

These are the types of confessions that lead one to experience transitions into each level. The phases of spiritual growth and the processes of the three levels of faith go on and on until we are complete in Him. God knows what the finished product will be. In Jesus we've seen the finished product. Yes, until we leave this planet we will have to beat our bodies under, as the apostle Paul says. Our bodies still have the tendencies to sin, but that is why we are going to drop these earthly bodies, which are programmed to sin. Our souls are being transformed into the image of God as we renew our minds to think in line with God's thoughts in the Scriptures. We mature by walking in God's royal law of love.

> Herein is our love made perfect, that we may have boldness in the day of judgment; because *as he is, so are we* in this world. (1 John 4:17)

One day, God will give us a new glorified body, which has no sin in it. Until that time spiritual growth is the process of learning about God, learning to walk with God, learning to fellowship with God, and perfecting the love of Christ, until our son-ship is complete. Just as we are born as babes and we must grow into children and mature as sons who can represent the family name and carry on the family business in the natural, even so it is in the spiritual. God's family is being enlarged with sons. Those who walk with God as sons will grow in faith and their son-ship will manifest the supernatural events that testify that God is with them.

You Can Be a Son

> He that believeth on the Son of God hath the witness in himself: he that believeth not God hath made him a liar; because he believeth

> not the record that God gave of his Son. And this is the record that
> God hath given to us eternal life, and this life is in his Son. He that
> hath the Son hath life; and he that hath not the Son of God hath not
> life. These things have I written unto you that believe on the name
> of the Son of God; that ye may know that ye have eternal life, and
> that ye may believe on the name of the Son of God. (1 John 5:10-13)

If you have the Son in you, then you have His life in you and you know you have the life because God has given you a witness in your heart that you are born of God. Jesus has conquered death for us and has become the portal into immortality. Jesus by His resurrection became the door through which we enter into fellowship with God for eternity. God wants us to know we already have eternal life and that His divine nature is living and growing in us. We are not only citizens of Heaven on earth but we are the lights of the world. True Christianity is not just living for Jesus, but it is living *by* Jesus. This is the message Jesus preached everywhere He went: "God is a Father and by me, you can be a son."

> For this corruptible must put on incorruption, and this mortal must
> put on immortality. So when this corruptible shall have put on in-
> corruption, and this mortal shall have put on immortality, then shall
> be brought to pass the saying that is written, Death is swallowed up
> in victory. (1 Cor. 15:53-54)

You can put on immortality as you live by Jesus Christ. That is the plan of God, the purpose of God, the wisdom of God, the love of God, and the secret of eternity. The theme of the Bible reveals God's eternal plan to expand His heavenly family by making more sons. This is more of an incentive for humans than forgiveness of sins and Heaven when we die. It's the life that was promised us before the world began. This lifestyle of Heaven is the fellowship of the heavenly Father and His sons. It's the heavenly Father gathering His sons for eternity. Faith is living by Jesus and doing the works of Jesus while we're here on earth until it's time to go to Heaven where Jesus is the King.

> For ye are all the children of God by faith in Christ Jesus. For as
> many of you as have been baptized into Christ have put on Christ.

There is neither Jew nor Greek, there is neither bond nor free, there is *neither male nor female*: for ye are all one in Christ Jesus. And if ye be Christ's, then are ye Abraham's seed, and heirs according to the promise. (Gal. 3:26-29)

You see, the life of Jesus wasn't just the best life ever lived by a human, male or female. His life was the life God meant for us to have, which was lost in the Garden of Eden. Do you remember the paradise of fellowship Adam had with God? Adam never took the next step of eating from the Tree of Life to receive His divine nature. Adam walked away from God and the life of immortality was lost. As a result, everyone born of Adam is born spiritually dead and alienated from the life of God. Jesus came to give it back to us. God sent Jesus to pay the penalty of our sins, take our punishment in Hell and to purchase pardon for us so we could come back to God as though we had never sinned. God now expects every believer to walk in fellowship with God and mature as the people of God. That is the life that is eternal.

For what shall it profit a man, if he shall gain the whole world, and lose his own soul? Or what shall a man give in exchange for his soul? (Mark 8:36-37)

You can live your whole life without God and be a success, but when you enter into eternity without God, it will be your ultimate failure and it will be forever. If you lose your soul, you will have lost everything. The only thing you can give in exchange for your soul is your heart. If you will invest in yourself and give God your heart, He will activate His power in your soul to become glorified in the Son.

Personal Study Notes

CHAPTER 10

THE SECRET *of* ETERNITY

For this cause I bow my knees unto the Father
of our Lord Jesus Christ, of whom the whole family
in heaven and earth is named.

EPH. 3:14-15

God Is Having a Family

> Having predestinated us unto the adoption of children by Jesus Christ to himself, . . . That in the dispensation of the fullness of times he might gather together in one all things in Christ, both which are in heaven, and which are on earth; even in him. (Eph. 1:3-14)

> Now therefore ye are no more strangers and foreigners, but fellow citizens with the saints, and of the household of God. (Eph. 2:19)

In the beginning of this book, I said the good news of the Bible is the revelation of God's purpose for creation to have an eternal family. *It is the good news of the heavenly provision, which a loving God has made through His only Son, to recover man out of the state of death into which he has fallen and to bring him back into the glorious state of life and fellowship, enlarging His heavenly family.* The purpose of God was always to have a family, and the message of the Bible for every human is, you can be a son. God has shown us in Jesus what His heavenly children look like and live like. God has demonstrated to us in Jesus what eternal life is. Eternal Life is a father and son walking in paradise forever. What is good for God is also good for us. That's the secret of eternity; God is having a family and *you* can be a son.

> For this cause I bow my knees unto the Father of our Lord Jesus Christ, Of whom the whole family in heaven and earth is named, that he would grant you, according to the riches of his glory, to be strengthened with might by his Spirit in the inner man; That Christ may dwell in your hearts by faith; that ye, being rooted and grounded in love, May be able to comprehend with all saints what is the breadth, and length, and depth, and height; And to know the love of Christ, which passeth knowledge, that ye might be filled with all the fullness of God. Now unto him that is able to do exceeding abundantly above all that we ask or think, according to the power that worketh in us. (Eph. 3:14-20)

Hopefully this book has helped you to gain insight into God's eternal program. In 2,000 years since the cross, the worldwide church has barely come to realize the gravity of what God has done through His Son, Jesus Christ. The scriptures clearly teach that Jesus is the firstborn from the dead and He is bringing many sons (brethren) unto glory. God in His wisdom is having an eternal family that He is going to enjoy forever. That is the secret of eternity. God is going to gather everyone in Heaven and Earth who is in His beloved family and He is going to spend eternity enjoying His family. It is as practical in the spiritual as it is in the natural. We do the same things with our families.

> Behold, what manner of love the Father hath bestowed upon us, that we should be called the sons of God: therefore the world knoweth us not, because it knew him not. Beloved, now are we the sons of God, and it doth not yet appear what we shall be: but we know that, when he shall appear, we shall be like him; for we shall see him as he is. And every man that hath this hope in him *purifieth himself, even as he is pure.* (1 John 3:1-3)

What we see in these passages of scripture is beyond our imagination. It is so incredible and so wonderful that it defies the natural mind of man. But God's plan was always to grow humans into His very own sons. Adam caused a setback in time for man, but Satan didn't cause a setback in eternity for God. He has blessed us *with all spiritual blessings* in heavenly places in Christ. The Bible says all of creation is learning right now the manifold wisdom of God through the unsearchable riches of Christ. That includes the angels. But the clue to how the secret of eternity will be completed in you and me is found in the last seven words of this passage of scripture. It won't just happen. We must *purify ourselves even as He is pure.* We are hoping that we might become full of His divine nature and walk with God the way Jesus did. With this hope we are purifying ourselves by putting off the old man with his deeds and putting on the new man who is filled with God's Spirit.

> But now ye also put off all these; anger, wrath, malice, blasphemy, filthy communication out of your mouth. Lie not one to another, seeing that ye have put off the old man with his deeds; And have

put on the new man, which is renewed in knowledge after the image of him that created him. (Col. 3:8-1)

This takes place over time as we grow just like kids grow in the natural. Our change of nature is something that is initiated by the Spirit of God and forcefully practiced by the human being as we mature spiritually. Jesus was the prototype and the demonstration of the finished eternal model. In Him are all the specs and features of the highest trim level of humanity in the universe that operates by the Spirit of God. He is what we are destined to become as we purify ourselves even as He is pure. We discuss this process of spiritual maturity in the next book in this series called *Death and Life, Secret of the Bible*. Our spiritual maturity affects the quality of our resurrection as well as our fruitfulness in life and in doing the works of Jesus while we are in this world.

The Grace of God

What we have learned in this book is:

God's
Riches
At
Christ's
Expense

It's impossible to fully comprehend the grace of God. Hopefully I've at least given you a clear view of the grace of God in this book. Simply put, the grace of God is the goodness of God. Grace is the heavenly provision of God's goodness towards you. It is everything He has done for you through Jesus Christ. You didn't deserve it. You couldn't earn it. God did it all for you because He loves you and He doesn't want you to perish. Jesus is the grace of God in human form. In Jesus we see the riches of Heaven and we see all of God's riches invested into the human race. Jesus took our death that we might live forever with Him. Resurrection is now guaranteed to all believers by the power of God. Through Jesus, God's love for you is clearly seen.

Wherefore I also, after I heard of your faith in the Lord Jesus, and love unto all the saints, Cease not to give thanks for you, making mention of you in my prayers; That the God of our Lord Jesus Christ, the Father of glory, may give unto you the spirit of wisdom and revelation in the knowledge of him: The eyes of your understanding being enlightened; that ye may know what is *the hope of his calling,* and what *the riches of the glory* of his inheritance in the saints, And what is the *exceeding greatness of his power* to us-ward who believe, according to the working of his mighty power, Which he wrought in Christ, when he raised him from the dead, and set him at his own right hand in the heavenly places, Far above all principality, and power, and might, and dominion, and every name that is named, not only in this world, but also in that which is to come: And hath put all things under his feet, and gave him to be the head over all things to the church, Which is his body, the fullness of him that filleth all in all. (Eph. 1:15-23)

Paul is asking God in this prayer to give us *the Spirit of Wisdom and Revelation* in the knowledge of God to open our eyes so we can know the truth and experience His power in our lives. I encourage you to pray this prayer for yourself daily that Paul prayed for believers in his day. Daniel prayed three times a day and kept himself clean in the presence of God and God was able to manifest Himself greatly for Daniel. We not only need to know about the world to come but we need to know how to walk with God in this present evil world that our lives might benefit others for their salvation and deliverance from evil.

I hope the goal of this book has been accomplished in you. It *was written to open the eyes* of your heart to see the secret of eternity, which God wants to reveal to all believers. Hopefully this book has provided enough insight for you to have all the information you need to make quality decisions about your eternal destiny. God planned before creation to enlarge His heavenly family. God knew everything that was going to happen after creation and He made plans through Jesus Christ to display and empower the provisions of the grace of God. It was wonderful that God would document everything in the Bible. It was incredible God told us beforehand that His Son would come and what His Son would do, but

God is still at work. God isn't finished. The final product is on the verge of being revealed.

By the grace of God Jesus became the heavenly provision that was promised. By the grace of God everyone is invited to be in God's heavenly family. Just like a good father makes provision for his children on the earth, even so God is the heavenly Father and He has made provision for everyone to be born again into God's family through Jesus Christ. Just like God walked with Jesus, He will walk with all His people who fellowship with Him. There will come a time when God will gather everyone on earth that is in His family together with everyone in Heaven. We will then spend eternity with the Lord. God's love will be the only law in existence. Just like humans who love one another get married and have a family to share that love, even so God is doing the same with us.

> Behold, what manner of love the Father hath bestowed upon us, that we should be called the sons of God: therefore the world knoweth us not, because it knew him not. (1 John 3:1)

The human family was started and designed by God to reveal His heavenly purpose of having a family. God is so big the universe is His garden, and yet the Bible says God fills all things. God knows all our thoughts, our motives, and our ways. Yet as little as we are in such a big universe, God loves us and cares for us. The Bible says we are so special to God that He has numbered the hairs on our head. The Bible says God is love. That is the big revelation of the Bible, God is love. This no mere religion teaches or even imagines. The Bible is the only source where we can find the love of God and experience it. The purpose of creation is that God is having a family with whom He can share His unlimited eternal love forever. He had one Son and He wanted more so He created the universe to serve as a foundation for the planet Earth. Then He created earth to give man a place to live. Then He created man in order to have a family. God has predestined that we be born of His divine nature through Christ in us and become the sons of God.

> That ye may be blameless and harmless, the sons of God, without rebuke, in the midst of a crooked and perverse nation, among whom ye shine as lights in the world. (Phil. 2:15)

God has not only purposed in His heart to reveal His Son, Jesus Christ from Heaven, but also to reveal His family of sons who are in Heaven and earth. I could also say sons and daughters of God, but the Bible doesn't see male and female in Heaven, but rather it says we are a new species of being that never existed before. What the Bible reveals is a new creature who has been redeemed out of earth and brought into His heavenly family and the Bible calls them the sons of God.

Whosoever Believeth

Jesus said unto her, I am the resurrection, and the life: he that believeth in me, though he were dead, yet shall he live: And whosoever liveth and believeth in me shall never die. Believest thou this? She saith unto him, Yea, Lord: I believe that thou art the Christ, the Son of God, which should come into the world. (John 11:25-27)

Truly no other man has ever spoken like Jesus. No other man has ever lived like Jesus nor has any man ever done the works and the miracles Jesus did. In all of human history, nobody else has ever said, "I am the resurrection and if you believe in me, even if you are dead you shall live." Only Jesus talked like this. Only Jesus went around loving and healing people of every disease. Only Jesus raised people from the dead. Only Jesus said, "Father, forgive them for they know not what they do." Only Jesus said, "I and my Father are one." Only Jesus left the tomb empty for all to see. Only Jesus, from the day He came into this world until the day He left, demonstrated the love of God and the power of God. History records that He has risen from the dead. There was only one virgin womb. There is only one empty tomb.

Jesus is asking you now, do you believe this?

Afterward he appeared unto the eleven as they sat at meat, and upbraided them with their unbelief and hardness of heart, because they believed not them which had seen him after he was risen. And he said unto them, Go ye into all the world, and preach the gospel to every creature. He that believeth and is baptized shall be saved;

but he that believeth not shall be damned. And *these signs shall follow them that believe*; In my name shall they cast out devils; they shall speak with new tongues; They shall take up serpents; and if they drink any deadly thing, it shall not hurt them; they shall lay hands on the sick, and they shall recover. (Mk. 16:14-18)

Jesus commanded believers to share the truth with others, and He said as we live and preach the gospel, certain signs of God's power will follow those in His family who truly believe. Those with Christ in them will do the same works and experience the same results Christ did. He said we will cast out devils in His name, we will speak with new tongues in His name, we shall take up serpents (devils) in His name, we shall lay hands on the sick in His name and they shall recover. Now that is strong faith. When Jesus said, ". . . they shall recover," He meant they shall go through a process of recovery until they are fully healed. A miracle is instantaneous, but recovery is a process. But that is what Jesus promised us if we have faith. Other religions may borrow some of the events and principles of the Bible but they don't have the love of God, the power to heal and authority to proclaim forgiveness of sins. This power only comes through believers in Christ. Jesus said if you believe in Him, then you will be saved, and if you won't believe in Him, then you will be damned.

Then the eleven disciples went away into Galilee, into a mountain where Jesus had appointed them. And when they saw him, they worshipped him: but some doubted. And Jesus came and spake unto them, saying, *All power is given unto me in heaven and in earth*. Go ye therefore, and teach all nations, baptizing them in the name of the Father, and of the Son, and of the Holy Ghost: Teaching them to observe all things whatsoever I have commanded you: and, lo, I am with you alway, even unto the end of the world. Amen. (Matt. 28:16-20)

Jesus said, ". . . all power in Heaven and Earth is given unto me. Go therefore in the power of my name and teach, and preach, heal, and deliver. All who will believe will be saved and all who won't believe will be damned." Jesus has never said anything that hasn't come to pass yet. Notice the power of the name of Jesus. Do you believe God has given Jesus all power in Heaven and Earth?

Again Jesus commands us to go into the entire world and teach all nations the truth. He said as we go He is with us always. He said *all power* is given unto Him in Heaven and in earth. That's a lot of power. The power of God is in the name of Jesus. Just like the name of a billionaire is enough to reap benefits to those who are related to him, even so all of Heaven stands behind the name of Jesus in earth. Our mission as believers while we are still on planet Earth is to walk in the power of God and release others from Satan's dominion of death and bring them into the Kingdom of God. We are royal ambassadors of the King of Heaven. In His name we experience the power of God.

> Verily I say unto you, Whatsoever ye shall bind on earth shall be bound in heaven: and whatsoever ye shall loose on earth shall be loosed in heaven. Again I say unto you, That if two of you shall agree on earth as touching anything that they shall ask, it shall be done for them of my Father which is in heaven. For where two or three are gathered together in my name, *there am I in the midst* of them. (Matt. 18:18-20)

Heaven has invaded earth and Heaven's authority flows through Jesus Christ. The Bible says, whatever we bind on earth *in the name* of Jesus is what is bound in Heaven. It means what we permit or allow on earth in His name is what is allowed in Heaven and what we don't permit or allow on earth in His name is not allowed in Heaven. Isn't it interesting that the name of Jesus who is in Heaven affects us on earth and what we do on earth in Jesus' name affects Heaven? Jesus said His name is the only name that we can call upon and get God's attention. When the name of Jesus is uttered, Heaven listens, angels are dispatched and devils tremble.

> Neither is there salvation in any other: for *there is none other name under heaven given among men*, whereby we must be saved. (Acts 4:12)

Other religions will enhance their authority by including Jesus in their philosophies, but the Bible says only the name of Jesus has all the authority of Heaven in Earth. The name of Jesus is the name that releases the power of God. We saw the power of God in Jesus' life. Everything Jesus did and said was filled with the power of God. We saw the power of God in Jesus' death. Every aspect of Jesus' death fulfilled the promises of the fathers and the prophecies of the prophets. We saw the power of God in Jesus' resurrection. His resurrection has been historically verified and never has been disproven. Jesus is alive and His power of God is distributed in His name through them that believe. With Jesus miracles never cease. However, the greatest miracle in the name of Jesus isn't healing or casting out devils, but it is *the new birth*. When God causes the new birth to happen in the name of Jesus, a new species of being that never existed before comes into being. When we come to God in the name of Jesus, the power of God that raised Him from the dead quickens us and causes us to be born again.

> But Jesus said unto them, With men this is impossible; but with God all things are possible. (Matt. 19:26)

> Jesus said unto him, If thou canst believe, all things are possible to him that believeth. (Mark 9:23)

The name of Jesus is the name of the one who is alive forevermore. The name of Jesus still has the power to heal us of our physical diseases. There is no other name that manifests the love of God and the power of God. No other name under Heaven can save us, heal us, change us, or deliver us from the powers of death. He loved us and He still loves us. When we call upon God in the name of Jesus, the power of God is released into us. The same Spirit who raised Jesus from the dead quickens our mortal bodies and makes us whole when we believe. In the name of Jesus, all the power of God is available to believers just like the power of the electric company is available to your home. But the power doesn't turn on the light bulb. The light switch turns on the light bulb. Faith is the light switch that turns on the power of God.

> Jesus saith unto him, I am the way, the truth, and the life: no man cometh unto the Father, but by me. (John 14:6-7)

God is pleased with Jesus. His resurrection proves that unto us. When we call upon God in the name of Jesus to save us, God is pleased with us and

He is pleased to give us eternal life. Eternal life is the gift of God. The moment we believe in Jesus, the Bible says we pass from death to life. The Bible says that as we mature spiritually we become royal ambassadors of Christ and embassies of Heaven.

The Condemnation

He that believeth on him is not condemned: but *he that believeth not is condemned already*, because he hath not believed in the name of the only begotten Son of God. And this is the condemnation, that light is come into the world, and *men loved darkness rather than light*, because their deeds were evil. For every one that doeth evil hateth the light, neither cometh to the light, lest his deeds should be reproved. But he that doeth truth cometh to the light, that his deeds may be made manifest, that they are wrought in God. (John 3:16-21)

The Bible says the only reason you stand condemned before God is because you haven't believed in the name of the only begotten Son of God. Jesus told everyone He is the Son of God. Jesus' life, death and resurrection prove that He is the Son of God. Jesus is the cornerstone that we can build our eternal house upon. Whatever life you build, it won't be an eternal house in Heaven without Jesus Christ as the cornerstone.

We are born as sinners in Adam before God, but when we call upon the name of Jesus, all condemnation before God goes away. Just as a baby has no past, even so the new creature has no past but stands righteous before God. The Bible says all one has to do to become saved is to believe the truth in Jesus. He that believeth on Him is not condemned but he that doesn't believe is already condemned. That is stout language. That is the Bible. If you truly believe, then God's goodness of salvation has already begun. Now that doesn't mean you are finished just because you are a believer and you are going to Heaven. After the new birth the Bible says we grow up into Him in all things and mature in His divine nature. According to the Bible, if you don't believe in Jesus, you are condemned already because you haven't believed in the name of the only begotten Son of God. Jesus was sent by God from Heaven to earth so we wouldn't be condemned. The Bible says the name of Jesus is the only name given under Heaven whereby men *must* be saved. There is no other name that has overcome death. There is no other name that has a resurrection power in it. There is no other name that reveals and demonstrates the power of God. There is no other name that has demonstrated the love of God.

> For whoso findeth me findeth life, and shall obtain favour of the LORD. But he that sinneth against me wrongeth his own soul: all they that hate me love death. (Prov. 8:35-36)

Those who don't believe in the name of Jesus stand condemned before God because they have refused the gift of God and have shown disrespect to the Son of God who laid down His life for us. It goes on to say that we are condemned because light has come into the world and we loved darkness rather than light. That is the condemnation. It says our deeds prove that we love darkness rather than the light. How do you know you love darkness rather than light? Because you hate the light? Do you hate the things of God or do you love the things of God? That is how you can tell whether you are in the darkness or the light. The scripture says those who do truth come to the light and go through the change so that they are living their lives and doing their deeds in the sight of God. We either hate God and the things of God or we love God and the things of God.

> *He that hateth me hateth my Father also.* If I had not done among them the works which none other man did, they had not had sin: but now have they both seen and hated both me and my Father. But this cometh to pass, that the word might be fulfilled that is written in their law, they hated me without a cause. (John 15:23-25)

Some people get offended when they see Jesus claimed to be God. They have a problem with Jesus calling Himself the Son of God. What's the problem? Jesus did things no other man has ever done, proving God was in Him. On three different occasions God spoke to the people out of

Heaven, saying, "This is my beloved Son in whom I am well pleased, hear ye Him." When God spoke from Heaven they said it was thunder. But Jesus said His father was testifying of Him. Everything Jesus taught and did was to teach us that God was His Father and He was God's Son, and He came from Heaven (sent by God) to save us and give us eternal life. How much more can you see the love of God? No religion on earth, created by man or angel, teaches or demonstrates the love of God. If Jesus wasn't raised from the dead by the power of God, then every human being is without hope *forever*.

Some people think, "Okay, if God loves everyone then He will save everyone. How can He let anyone go to Hell?" The truth is, God doesn't want anyone to go to Hell and He doesn't send anyone to Hell. He has provided the supernatural power to bring every soul on earth to Heaven, but the power of God doesn't work until we activate it in our hearts by faith. If we love this present world more than God and refuse to activate His supernatural power within our hearts by faith, we send ourselves to Hell. We have no business going there. God made it possible through Jesus Christ that we don't have to go to there.

The Bible teaches Satan is the one who brought the human race under the dominion of death. People stand condemned before God when they love darkness rather than light and choose not to receive God's gift of eternal life, which He offers unto us through Jesus Christ. Hell is the eternal abode of Satan and his kids. By believing in Jesus, we become the children of God. Heaven is the eternal abode of God and His kids. In John 3:16-21, we see what is the thing that condemns the human before God. It says, "light has come into the world and men loved darkness rather than light, because their deeds were evil."

What condemns the human isn't how bad he is, just like what saves the human isn't how good he is. What condemns us is that God has shown us the spiritual and we love the natural rather than the spiritual. God has shined His light into our hearts with the *Truth of Eternity* and we love this temporary *see and be seen world* rather than the world to come. Jesus came from Heaven to earth to show us the life and we loved death rather than life. The light of truth came through the words of Jesus and we loved darkness rather than light. What proves this to be true is, our deeds are evil.

> But he that doeth truth cometh to the light, that his deeds may be made manifest, that they are wrought in God. (John 3:21)

What is darkness? it is living life without God? What is evil? Is it being your own god? God has shined the light of the *Truth for Eternity* into this world through His only Son and men loved living life without God and using the *self program* to be their own gods. The Scripture says our deeds prove whether we love darkness rather than light. It goes on to say, everyone that does evil hates the light and won't come to the light so that their deeds (way of life) should be changed before God.

> A new heart also will I give you, and a new spirit will I put within you: and I will take away the stony heart out of your flesh, and I will give you an heart of flesh. (Ezek. 36:26)

The Bible says when we call upon the name of Jesus *we are saved* by the power of God. God gives us a new spirit, making us fit to live in Heaven, and a new heart that loves the things of God. Those who love the light determine in their hearts to do the truth. They walk in the light that their deeds may be made manifest that they are being wrought in the Spirit of God. This is so profound. Many have heard the passage of John 3:16 but not many have heard the rest of that passage that shows God has a proving system when we come to Him. Those who are truly born again purpose in their heart to do the truth, living by Jesus instead of Adam. My deeds prove whether I am living by Adam or by Jesus. For example, when Adam's lust in the man's flesh tells him, look over there at that woman, and he says, "no, I don't obey you anymore," his flesh begins to learn to disobey its lusts. His deeds prove that he loves light rather than darkness because he is overcoming the addictions of lust through Christ in him. When his flesh says, "smoke that cigarette," and he says, "no, I don't obey you anymore," his deeds are being made manifest that they are being wrought in God instead of his flesh nature. These are just a few examples of dying unto self that we might live unto God.

> And he said to them all, If any man will come after me, let him deny himself, and take up his cross daily, and follow me. (Luke 9:23)

To go from death to life, I must take up my cross in Christ and lay down my life in Adam, so I can live by the life of the Son who loved me and gave Himself for me. I purpose to do truth until the ways of my body are manifesting in Christ. I purpose in my heart to do all things through Christ in me that I might walk with the Father. In this way I am able to see that all my deeds are being wrought in the presence of God my heavenly Father. When I mess up I come to God and repent and ask for forgiveness so I can walk in the light again.

If you believe the gospel that God has forgiven you of your sins, that you are going to Heaven and that you are a child of God, then you are coming to the light and walking in the light, with the motive of doing what Adam failed to do. Your purpose is to overcome all things of Adam so that everything you do is being wrought in God through Christ *in* you. The Bible says our purpose is that all our deeds may be made manifest that we are doing them in Christ and not in Adam. Through Christ in us we do the deeds of our heavenly Father just like Jesus did the deeds of the heavenly Father. That is the eternal lifestyle Jesus taught and demonstrated. Our goal as born again believers is to not live by the first man Adam, but to live by the second man Jesus who indwells us. The Bible says in Colossians 3:4, "He is our life."

> Moreover, brethren, I declare unto you the gospel which I preached unto you, which also ye have received, and wherein ye stand; By which also ye are saved, if ye keep in memory what I preached unto you, unless ye have believed in vain. (1 Cor. 15:1-2)

There are those who believe they are saved, but they are not. The Bible is trying to help us make sure we have truly believed. It isn't that I just believe Jesus died on the cross. The Bible says the devils believe in God and they tremble. I must believe to the point that it changes my spiritual nature. I must believe in the love of God, but I must also believe in the power of God. I must come to God and enter into a love relationship with Him. I come to God believing in His goodness toward me and in His provision for me. I believe that God loved me and gave His Son, Jesus, to be my Savior so He could take my place in judgment and give me His Spirit and His righteous standing before God. He has demonstrated His love for you through His only Son, and God's love demands a response. How do you respond?

I am crucified with Christ: nevertheless I live; *yet not I, but Christ liveth in me*: and the life which I now live in the flesh I live by the faith of the Son of God, who loved me, and gave himself for me. (Gal. 2:20)

As a son, I must believe that He is always with me, that I do nothing without Him, that He works through me and the Father is with me. I must believe that it is no longer I who live, but Christ lives in me and the life I now live, I live by the faith of the one who loved me and gave Himself for me. I am learning to believe that as a son I do the works of Jesus and when I utter the name of Jesus, things come to pass. When I truly come to God in faith, I not only believe what He has done for me, but I also believe in what my heavenly Father is doing through me. I submit myself to the Father of Spirits and become subject to His approval, His correction, His supervision, and His participation in my life. I must follow His instructions and allow His truth to change me as a person in my inward parts. In this way I ensure that I truly believe the truth of the Bible and love the light of God's presence rather than the darkness of life without God. If I truly come to God and walk with God in the light (of His presence), I will begin to love God and my deeds will begin to change. This proves that I am a true believer. That doesn't mean believers become perfect. It doesn't mean we can't be deceived or do things that are wrong. When God looks at our hearts, He can tell if we truly believe His words and if we love darkness rather than light.

It's not God's fault if we miss Heaven. It's also not God's fault if we miss living the Father and Son lifestyle of eternity, which Jesus taught and demonstrated while He was here on earth. But we should be able to judge for ourselves. We should be brutally honest with ourselves and ask ourselves questions that challenge us to purify ourselves even as He is pure. Do I love the things of God? Do I hate the selfishness of lust? Do I desire to get the lust out? Do I desire to be deceived no more? Do I humble myself under the mighty hand of God? Do I recognize the whole world system is based on the lie that we can be our own gods and live life without God?

For he is our God; and we are the people of his pasture, and the sheep of his hand. Today if ye will hear his voice, Harden not your heart. (Ps. 95:7-8)

The Bible has made all things clear that God has made provision for you. God has put you in position to receive eternal life through His only Son, Jesus Christ. If you will turn your heart to Him, He will quicken you by His Spirit and open your eyes to the *truth*.

> And, behold, I come quickly; and my reward is with me, to give every man according as his work shall be. (Rev. 22:12)

> He which testifieth these things saith, Surely I come quickly. Amen. Even so, come, Lord Jesus. (Rev. 22:20)

Remember the Three Issues of the Bible

1. Your Sins Are Gone

God's not holding one sin against you. God will never be mad at you one day of your life. He has promised to remember your sins no more. The Bible says in Isaiah 1:18, "Even though your sins are as scarlet, to God they are as white as snow." The Bible says, as far as the east is from the west, God has made your sins to be far from Him. The Lamb of God has taken away the sins of the world. The only sin God will hold against any human being is the rejection of His wonderful gift of eternal life through Jesus. To God that is the same as being guilty of the murder of Jesus. To God, no response is a *no* response.

2. You Must Be Born Again

It's only through receiving Christ in your heart that you receive His Spirit, which imparts to you His divine nature. Without His divine nature you cannot enter the Kingdom of God. This is the life you were meant to have but was lost for us by Adam, in the Garden of Eden. God sent His Son to be our Lamb of God and to remove our sins from us. Because of the goodness of God, we can go to the next phase of spiritual development and be born again of His divine nature.

3. You Can Be a Son

This is God's purpose for creating you. This is the reason why Jesus died on the cross and went to Hell for you. It's also the reason Jesus rose again for you. As the greater one indwells you, your destiny is to become like Him, in every way without any trace of sin, with the ability to walk in fellowship with the Father for eternity. As a son we grow and mature as we learn to do all things to please the Father and we do it for the good of others. Jesus said, "No one can come to the Father but by Him." Receiving Jesus and living by Him brings you into the lifestyle of miracles, signs, and wonders. The Bible says, *for you to live is Christ.* The Bible tells us *as He is so are we* in this present world. The Bible says, "In Him you live, move, and have your being."

I said in the beginning there is a greater incentive in the Bible than just forgiveness of sins and Heaven when you die. The secret of eternity is you can be a son. Many believers don't go far enough into their faith to believe that. Many believers settle with forgiveness of sins and Heaven when they die, but the goodness of God goes far beyond that.

Pray to God.

> Neither pray I for these alone, but for them also which shall believe on me through their word; That they all may be one; as thou, Father, art in me, and I in thee, that they also may be one in us: that the world may believe that thou hast sent me. And the glory which thou gavest me I have given them; that they may be one, even as we are one: I in them, and thou in me, that they may be made perfect in one; and that the world may know that thou hast sent me, and hast loved them, as thou hast loved me. (John 17:20-23)

Jesus has also prayed for you that you may experience the same oneness with the heavenly Father He has. Jesus has asked God to love you the same way He loves Jesus. Jesus has asked God to give you the same glory He enjoys in His walk with God. God has promised us that what He has begun in us He will perfect in us until the perfect day. The life that was lost God has restored unto you through Christ in you. Each and every day is now a moment in eternity where we are growing up into the sons of God.

> But if we walk in the light, as he is in the light, we have fellowship one with another, and the blood of Jesus Christ his Son cleanseth us from all sin. (1 John 1:7)

If you are walking with God and you are experiencing success by overcoming the world, the flesh and the devil, you are on your way to son-ship. However, when we fail, and we will, we have an advocate with the Father who is our high priest, and just as He represents God to us, He also represents us to the Father. God doesn't see you but He sees Christ in you and He is very pleased. But when we sin, and we will, the blood of Jesus is the heavenly provision whereby we may be cleansed from all sin and get right back into fellowship with the heavenly Father. As you pray you could say words similar to this:

Heavenly Father,

I acknowledge your goodness towards me and I receive your heavenly provision. I receive Jesus Christ as my savior and Lord. Thank you for sending your only Son, Jesus, to be my innocent sacrificial Lamb of God. Thank you for giving Him to become my substitute in death. I now understand that He is my substitute in life. Teach me, heavenly Father, how to walk by faith and live by Jesus Christ, which is pleasing unto you. I trust that everything Jesus did perfectly satisfies your divine justice under the Law of God and that I am now a citizen of Heaven. Teach me how to be a son unto you without any trace of sin. Train me how to grow up into Him in all things as I walk with you. Teach me how to submit to the Father of spirits so I can live and move and have my being in Christ.

Cleanse me, heavenly Father, with the precious blood of Jesus from all unrighteousness, from all uncleanness, from all carnality, from all filthiness of flesh and spirit, from every spot or wrinkle or any such thing, within and without, from head to toe, spirit, soul and body. Create in me a clean heart and renew in me a right spirit. Let the meditations of my heart be acceptable in your sight. Let all the deeds of my body be made manifest that they are wrought in God. I will walk with you in the light and be led of you by your Spirit until it is time to come to your heavenly nity.

In Jesus' name I pray, Amen.

Jesus,

Come into my heart and be my Lord. Thank you for laying down your life for me that I might live forever in Heaven with you. Thank you for loving me before I was born. I open the door of my heart and ask you to come into my life. I trust in you as my Lord and Savior and I believe God has reconciled me to Himself through your death upon the cross. I believe God has raised you from the dead and I put my trust in you to bring me into your city of Heaven. I believe this moment that you come into me and save me and fill me with your Spirit so I can walk with the heavenly Father in all the affairs of life. I now choose to walk with the Father each day and depend upon Him in all things. I believe the Father will grow me up into His very own son. Jesus, fill me with your Spirit, lead me by your Spirit and train me to walk in the ways of life.

In your name, Jesus, I pray, Amen.

> But if the Spirit of him that raised up Jesus from the dead dwell in you, he that raised up Christ from the dead *shall also quicken your mortal bodies by his Spirit* that dwelleth in you. (Rom. 8:11)

God has promised you citizenship in Heaven as a believer in Jesus Christ. He has promised to walk with you on earth and meet all your needs according to His riches in glory by Christ in you. Jesus is alive and He sits at the right hand of God interceding for you. He is the heir of all things and He has prepared a place for you in Heaven. I look forward to seeing you there!

> Lay not up for yourselves treasures on earth, where moth and rust destroy and where thieves break in and steal; but lay up for yourselves treasures in heaven, where neither moth nor rust destroys and where thieves do not break in and steal. For where your treasure is, there your heart will be also. (Matt. 6:19-21 NKJV)

To open their eyes, and to turn them from darkness to light, and from the power of Satan unto God, that they may receive forgiveness of sins, and inheritance among them, which are sanctified by faith that is in me. (Acts 26:18)

This book is the first volume in a five book series called the Secrets of the Bible series. Each book in the series presents a stage of spiritual growth addressed in Acts 26:18. If this book has accomplished its goal of opening your eyes, we would like to hear from you. Feel free to contact us at www.truthforeternity.com

Personal Study Notes

Secrets of the Bible Series

BY STEVEN AND BONNIE MOORE